# Coniston Copper Mines

### A FIELD GUIDE
### TO THE MINES IN THE
### COPPER ORE FIELD
### AT CONISTON
### IN THE ENGLISH LAKE DISTRICT

ERIC G. HOLLAND

*Illustrations by the author.*

cp

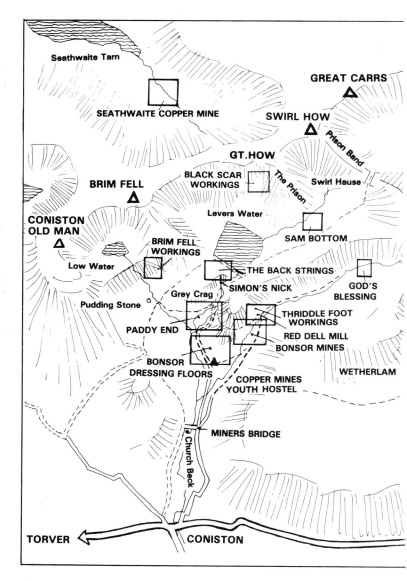

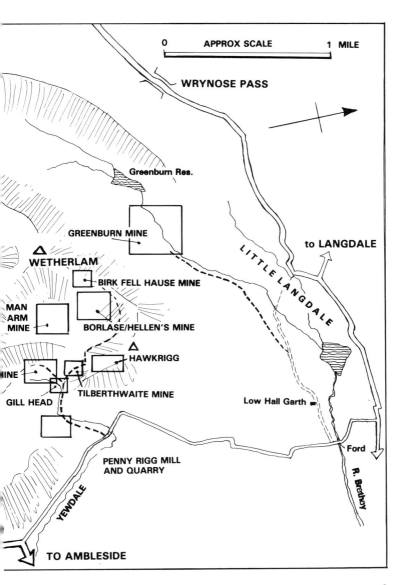

0   APPROX SCALE   1   MILE

WRYNOSE PASS

Greenburn Res.

GREENBURN MINE

to LANGDALE

LITTLE LANGDALE

△
WETHERLAM

BIRK FELL HAUSE MINE

MAN
ARM
MINE

BORLASE/HELLEN'S MINE

△
HAWKRIGG

...INE

TILBERTHWAITE MINE

GILL HEAD

Low Hall Garth

Ford

PENNY RIGG MILL
AND QUARRY

R. Brathay

YEWDALE

TO AMBLESIDE

3

© *Eric G. Holland 1981*
*Cicerone Press, Milnthorpe, Cumbria*

*First published 1981*
*Reprinted 1982, 1986, 1989, 2000 (with amendments)*
*ISBN 0 902363 36 0*

*Front Cover:*
*Looking towards Paddy End and Simon's Nick*
*Photo: R.B.Evans*

*Back Cover:*
*The entrance to Cobbler's Level. Note that the explorer*
*is merely examining the entrance.*
*For further penetration into the level*
*he would put his helmet on!*
*Photo: R.B.Evans*


## WARNING

**All old mine workings are potentially dangerous. In this book the author has noted places of special danger but great caution is needed at all times.**

# Contents

# 1. Introduction

This is a field guide to the relics of copper mining in the fells above Coniston, at Tilberthwaite, Greenburn, and at Seathwaite Tarn above the Duddon Valley.

Though some may find the guidebook alone is sufficient the visitor is urged to arm him/herself with copies of Ordnance Survey sheets SD 29 NE., NY 20 SE., and NY 30 SW. These are of scale 6 ins. to the mile or 1:10,560. Larger scale maps are sure to be fine but smaller scales tend not to be clear enough for detailed exploration.

Poets and writers alike have often praised the grand mountainous scenery of Coniston but apart from a few historians such as Collingwood and Rawnsley they disregarded the endeavours of the 'old men' and their subterranean labour. Surely it can be held that the mining industry (and bear in mind that its beginnings are lost in the mists of time) adds a further dimension to the scenario and dare it be said, spice for the adventurous. Enter some of the galleries in the Coniston Fells and one is at once taken back almost 300 years in time.... further still in other places.

The visitor who deprecates the small amount of environmental disturbance caused by mining often fails to recognise the increasing, and lasting, damage done by tourism. Lakeland has long been an industrial area; many minerals have been mined and some smelted here. Of course the extractive industry is now but a shadow of its former self but old mining sites, (even the slate quarries) are undeniably a part of Lakeland's rich pageant.

Because of opportunities these old mine sites present for the study of industrial archaeology, for adventure, mineral collecting, geology etc., there is an ever increasing awareness being demonstrated by widely varying sections of the public. One could say, a new sport has come into being as more and more persons of all age groups, not contenting themselves solely with surface exploration and fossicking in old dumps, are going below ground. Undoubtedly people unfamiliar with old mines (or caves for that matter) are entering old workings and putting themselves unwittingly at risk. In the meantime mountain rescue teams are wisely equipping themselves for undergound rescue.

It is not the express intention of this book to *advise* the reader to enter old mineworkings. Of course many do - how else do the names of fools appear on tunnel walls in paint or smoke from carbide lamps? How else the needless rubbish strewn along the floors?

Note has been made of the workings that the writer considers *safe*. *Safe, however, is purely relative and it must be pointed out that inept behaviour, even in these safe workings, can give rise to danger*. This cannot be underestimated! Large parties of children below ground in the charge of too few teachers (possibly themselves inexperienced) are potentially in danger.

To minimise the risk of accident, explorers should wear helmets and have reliable lighting, preferably fitted to the helmet in order that the hands be free. Cheap plastic torches just will *not* do. Footwear should have good treads on the soles. Details of the intended trip should be left with someone in case of non-return. If going below ground it is a good thing to leave some form of indication at the entrance. If electron ladders are to be used, do not scorn a lifeline. Single rope technique is too expansive a subject to enter into here. Absolute care should be taken with the ropes and they should be inspected regularly. Old timber is always suspect and in certain workings the floors of tunnels have been mined away and replaced with wood .... they are thus false! It is advisable to join a club or society and it is surprising how much can be achieved if one does so. Much of this is common sense and in the end it is up to the individual. Mine exploration has a pretty clean record - let's keep it so.

There is one other point of note. This guide directs the visitor high into the fells. Conditions can be treacherous at high altitudes, especially in the colder months, even when the valley bottoms are pleasant. The reader is therefore well advised to take heed of the advice given to fell-walkers with reference to protective clothing.

Obey the country code.

*E.G.Holland,*
*Old Stainton Hall*
*1981*

# 2. Historical Sketch

Mining, by all accounts, commenced at Coniston in or around 1599 and there is no evidence that there was any activity prior to that date. A reporter of the period stated that the veins had been found by poor shepherds tending their sheep and through torrents of water during storms uncovering veins previously hidden. Early miners appear to have been Germans from Schwaz and Innsbruck districts of the Tyrol who were brought over by the Elizabethan 'Company of Mines Royal'.

Working commenced almost always upon the veins where they outcropped on the surface. As these deepened it became increasingly harder to wind up the ore and to bale out the water. Early in the 17th. Century, therefore, tunnels began to be driven in, to connect with the deepening workings from the surface, to effect drainage and to allow ore to be carried out in leather shoulder bags.

These early tunnels pre-date gunpowder and were driven, (as the ore was mined) with a variety of iron tools and wedges. Often fire was used to heat the rock which was then doused with cold water, mixed it is said, with vinegar. The sudden contractions in the rock caused spalling and fracturing, but the rock, even only cracked to a depth of one inch or less, was more readily workable with the crude implements available. Tunnels driven in by the 'old men' are frequently coffin-shaped in cross-section - narrow for the head, wider for the shoulders and tapering towards the bottom. The writer has entered coffin-levels of only 4ft 6ins in height, 6ins wide at the top widening to about 2ft and tapering down to about 12 inches. At Coniston they have been modified by later operators.

By the mid 17th Century the German miners at Coniston had taken their workings down, in places, over 200ft.

Towards the end of the 18th Century the Macclesfield Copper Company had taken the Bonsor or Coniston Mine well down, under the German workings, to some 575 ft from surface, with ore being extracted along a length of 600 or 700 feet. Winding and pumping was performed by waterwheel powered winch.

Early in the 19th Century the mine was developed by the famous John Taylor and the new levels, including the important Deep or Horse Level, were started in order to work new veins and others in greater depth. Shafts were sunk, including the fine Old Engine Shaft, Thriddle Shaft, New Engine Shaft and the Paddy End Engine Shaft.

Taylor withdrew and the name of Cornishman John Barrett became widely associated with the mine. It was in its heyday during the mid-1800's with several hundred people deriving a living from it. Many of these were Irishmen who came, not only from their homeland, but from other mining fields. By the end of the Century the mines had reached the respectable depth of over 205 fathoms (1,230 feet) from the Deep Adit Level, with, in places, some 600 feet, or more, of workings above adit.

Mining did not cease completely in the region until 1942 with the liquidation of the Greenburn & Tilberthwaite Mining Company. More recently (1954) an attempt to re-open the mines at Bonsor and Paddy End was made, by McKechnie Bros. Ltd., under the supervision of W.T.Shaw.

Evidence of working from the earliest times right through to the 1950's are to be seen at Coniston, thus creating a unique memorial to the immense endeavour which has taken place both on and under these fells. Every fragment on the extensive spoil-heaps, has been held in someone's hand, glanced at with a practiced eye - and rejected.

The Ancient Monuments branch of the Dept. of the Environment has seen fit to schedule the area around Coppermines House, (the Youth Hostel), formerly the mine office, as an area of historical and scientific interest.

# 3. Pumping out the water

Notes on pumping might at first appear to be somewhat superfluous in a guide of this nature but to state simply 'it is pumped out', scarcely stimulates the imagination! A further reason for providing them is that certain features relating to pumping and drainage are frequently mentioned. It is therefore desirable that the reader should have at least a working knowledge of these - especially the colloquialisms.

To the 16th and 17th Century miners water must have been something of a headache. Their workings consisted of open excavations on the veins where these outcropped to the surface, and although they dug trenches on the high side of their works in order to drain as much as possible away, nevertheless they could never completely prevent its ingress. So it need come as no surprise that in wet periods up to half a working day was often spent baling out the water which had accumulated over-night. Water (and of course ore) would likely at first have been lifted out, in leather or wooden buckets, by hand .... hand-over-hand until the working had deepened sufficiently to install a wooden windlass or jack-roll. (see Fig.2) Even with this simple machine lifting is quite slow and laborious and quite possibly, at some stage, a 'rag-and-chain' pump might have been put in. The early miners from the Tyrol used them in their other mines so would hardly have been unaware of their potential at Coniston.

A pump of this type was a simple, if not very efficient, device for lifting water. A continuous chain, fitted with plugs or knobs of strong shag perhaps reinforced with leather, passed through a vertical wooden pipe (often bored from a solid tree trunk) which had its lower end immersed in a sump which collected the water. The chain passed around the periphery of a wooden wheel at the top. This might be turned by water-wheel, or horse, though it was quite common to use men. Up to six men were required in a shift to work a pump of only 4 inches diameter and the work was exceedingly strenuous even when the lift was only twenty feet or so. The machine was clearly quite expensive to operate. If more than one lift was needed the lowest pump discharged into a cistern feeding the pump above. Eventually recourse was made to the arduous and lengthy task of driving drainage adits. Yet the rag-and-chain pump did not disappear from the mining scene for many years and later examples

*Fig. 2      Windlass or Jack-Roll*

were cast from iron.

When a tunnel or level was driven into a mountain-side it was normal practice to allow a slight up-gradient. This not only assisted in tramming out the loaded ore wagons, or indeed wheel-barrows for that matter, but also allowed the water to drain out naturally. A level such as this was known as an 'adit'. It will be apparent that, with a few exceptions, levels were driven in to reach known veins .... the angle of intersection being anything up to 90 degrees. In such a case the level is known as a cross-cut and if it also drains the working then it is also an adit. The tunnel is usually taken left and right along the vein (if only to try it) and this is then a working horizon or level. Any workings, i.e. stopes or sub. levels, above an adit are known as the 'backs' and these are self-draining. As a consequence they will never be prone to serious water difficulties - there will be no need for pumping.

Most of these hill mines, Coniston being no exception, have a lowest adit which is the most important one. Often it will be named the Horse Level or the Deep Adit Level - but it will invariably be the lowest which can be conveniently or economically put in. Frequently they run in for miles. There may be several hundreds of feet of stopes

11

above it but these will often all drain down into it and they are collectively known as its 'backs'.

When a mine begins to develop *below* its adit, problems with water will arise, for it will naturally accumulate in the bottoms of these 'under-hand' stopes *and shafts* which are ever deepening. It was the practice at Coniston (in the 1800's) to clay seal the false floors of levels which ran with water, in order to prevent it, so far as possible, from working its way down to the excavations below. (See Fig. 3). *Unfortunately this now constitutes a hazard in contemporary exploration for there is often no indication of a hollow floor - or the state of the wood holding it up.* It was never possible to prevent all water from percolating down; in every mine there are, after all, innumerable natural fissures, each a conduit for water, and notwithstanding the success in keeping some of the water out, pumping was invariably resorted to in the end.

The first heavy iron pumps at Coniston Mine appear to have been installed in the 1700's by the Macclesfield Company in their Bonsor East and West Shafts. Unfortunately no record of the make survives. A mechanical pump (water-powered) was working in Muckle Gill at the Tilberthwaite Mine in the early 19th Century and this might well have been a rag-and-chain unit in a shallow shaft. The earlier pumps at Coniston worked through much of the 18th century until replaced by more up-to-date and powerful units, put in by later adventurers, and these kept the mine dry until closure of the Deep Bottoms in the 1890's. There was a similar pump in the Engine Shaft at Greenburn Mine.

So great was the extent of the working on the Bonsor vein under the adit that when the pumps were at last stopped, it took three years to fill up. It must be pointed out, however, taking into account the area of workings drained by the Deep Adit, the make-of-water was, and indeed still is, remarkably small. Almost all the mine water emerges from Deep Adit Level mouth.

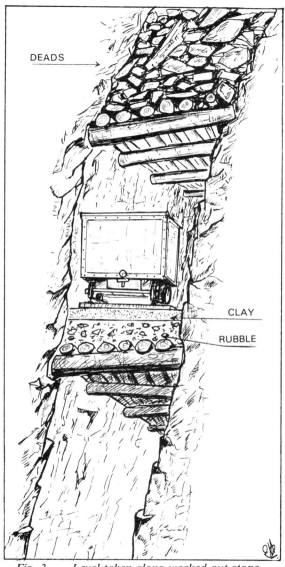

DEADS

CLAY

RUBBLE

*Fig. 3    Level taken along worked out stope.*

13

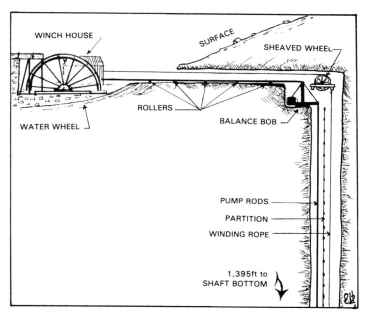

*Fig. 4    Section showing the Winding and Pumping arrangement at the top of 'Old Engine Shaft'.*

The pumping and winding arrangement at the Old Engine Shaft is diagrammatically illustrated in the simple sketch Fig. 4. This was the main pumping shaft at Coniston, the plunger pumps being situated on the 170 Fathom Level - 1,020 feet below adit or approx. 1,395 feet below surface. A bucket-lift/suction pump lifted the water from the 205 Level up to the 170.

Reciprocating motion for the pumps was provided by a crank on the water-wheel axle or winch and was transmitted to the pumps by an enormous 'rod' consisting of baulks or beams of wood strapped and bolted together. These ran firstly to the 'bishop's head' casting on a strange rocking device which converted the horizontal motion to vertical. The rod continued, hung from the 'nose' casting of the contraption, which was called a 'balance-bob', down the shaft (running through guides) to the pumps.

In the bottom of the mine the bucket-lift raised the water up to the

14

170 Level, on the up-stroke of the balance-bob. The main pump (a plunger H-piece set) worked on the down-stroke. The weight of the rod and its iron-work was, however, far superior to the water column in the iron rising-main pipe and it was this surplus of weight which pushed the water, through a clack-valve in the H-piece, up the rising-main. To reduce the effort of the water-wheel and prevent the entire thing from shuddering itself to pieces, the excess weight was counter-balanced by a weight-box on the balance-bob which was sufficiently loaded with rock or pieces of iron.

It can be seen from Fig. 4, that the head of the shaft was under-ground and that the balance-bob was seated in a special recess cut out in the rock for it - the 'bob-plat' (plat being an abbreviation for platform). The bob at the Old Engine Shaft lies in decayed ruin. There was a similar arrangement at the Thriddle Shaft but there the bob - albeit shorn of its castings - still stands as a sentinel to times past, awaiting the onset of total decay. This is shown in Fig. 5, whilst illustration Fig. 6 reconstructs the unit.

*Fig. 6      Thriddle Shaft Balance-Bob re-constructed.*

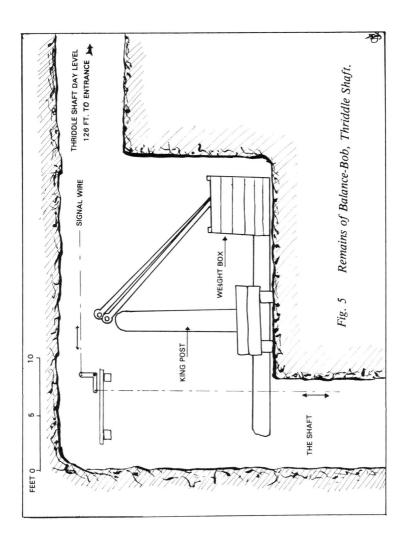

THRIDDLE SHAFT DAY LEVEL
126 FT. TO ENTRANCE

SIGNAL WIRE

WEIGHT BOX

KING POST

THE SHAFT

FEET 0   5   10

Fig. 5   Remains of Balance-Bob, Thriddle Shaft.

16

Decayed remnants of the bob are to be seen at Greenburn Mine. At Paddy End, in the absence of any record of pumping machinery, it can be assumed that the water, from the 20 Fathom Level (below Deep Adit Level there), was lifted as needed by kibble or skip up to the adit where it would have been poured away to run the 1½ miles or so to daylight.

# 4. Geological Outline

The rocks of the district consist of rhyolitic and andesite lava flows interbedded with hardened and cleaved volcanic dust and ashes and quite heavily faulted. The rhyolites are extremely hard and 'flinty'. The visitor, overawed perhaps by the crags and mountains in the area we shall cover with this guide, may not at first comprehend that they are all the product of past volcanic activity - on an enormous scale.

Hardened and cleaved dark, almost black, mudstones are also to be found in the region and these have been extensively wrought in the past for building material and flooring slabs. The ashes and tuffs are often well cleaved and have been quarried to an even greater extent for roofing slates, building stone, flooring slabs and so on. 'Slate' is still worked in the vicinity. Although flooring slabs (known locally as flag-stones) are quite common hereabouts yet probably the best example of 'slate' flags are to be seen in the bar of the Newfield Inn at Seathwaite in the Duddon Valley.

It appears that mineralisation from deep seated sources was chiefly confined to the harder rocks, and veins soon failed on passing through into softer country. It suggests that the cleaner fault fractures in the hard strata, which occured prior to or during the mineralisation period, allowed freer access to the ascending mineral rich solutions and vapours, whereas the fissures in the softer ground (the tuffs and ashes) would be more likely to be choked to a greater degree by fault debris.

The non-metallic vein filling consisted usually of shattered country-rock cemented with quartz. Dolomite, calcite and barytes have been recorded. Magnetite, the magnetic iron ore, came in in depth, in the Bonsor Vein in large amounts but at the expense of the copper. Other metallic minerals found were iron-pyrites, arsenopyrite or mispickel and of course the main one, sulphide of copper, chalcopyrite, which is itself invariably compounded with iron sulphide. Small amounts of nickel and cobalt have been found.

Coloured secondary products of the copper sulphide occurred in the oxidised upper zones of certain of the veins and azurite, the carbonate, and chrysocolla were worked in small amounts in the Levers Water region during the 17th Century though chiefly from surface workings. Some cuprite (the oxide) has been worked.

The copper ore was found disseminated amongst the vein filling as splashes and strings but also as veins or ribs of pure solid chalcopyrite suitable for marketing without any treatment other than reduction in size. In rich parts of the mines the veins carried solid ore which thickened at intersections with other veins or cross-faults. Often these 'bunches' were very rich and of considerable size; one such being the Californian Bunch at the intersection of Belman's Hole and Paddy End Veins.

The most important veins in the Coniston Mines are the Bonsor and Paddy End Veins and the latter, as well as being the most important in that portion of the mine known as Paddy or Paddy's End, was of more significance in that it carried richer ore than the Bonsor. The nomenclature of the veins at Paddy End is confused. Operators and miners at different periods have bestowed differing titles to the same veins and even similar names to more than one vein! Here at Paddy End, up near Levers Water, the main vein runs into a complexity of subsidiary lodes known collectively in the last century as the Back Strings (see Fig. 7). The vein pattern at outcrop bears little relationship to the structure in depth. Here can be found the main Paddy End with its branch Belman's Hole Vein, South Lode, New South Vein, Paddy End Old Vein, Stephen's Vein, New Vein, Jenkinson's and Parke's and Paddy Lodes, and a little apart from all these - Brimfell Vein.

These outcrop workings up near Levers Water appear an easy enough matter to descend but they are **EXTREMELY UNSAFE** to explore. Their 'floors' are really rubble covered decaying timbers, and below them the old stopes fall for hundreds of feet. **Content yourself by LOOKING ONLY at this most absorbing and ancient part of the workings.**

Other lodes at Coniston are the Thriddle (believed to be a section of the Bonsor); Kernal* vein which had two levels driven into it; one which really carried hardly any ore - Dry Gill Vein, and God's Blessing (writer). Tilberthwaite, Greenburn and Seathwaite all have their own groups of veins. To list them will be needless duplicity as they are all referred to in the appropriate sections of this book.

Veins in this ore-field generally strike NW-SE but are intersected and shifted by numerous faults which cut across almost at right angles. These are not themselves normally mineralised save at certain junctions. Two major faults, or cross-courses, which have a great

* *'Kernal' is the correct name according to local usage, although current O.S. maps show this as 'Kennel'.*

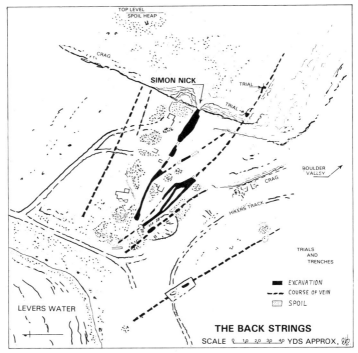

Labels within image: TOP LEVEL SPOIL HEAP, CRAG, SIMON NICK, TRIAL, TRIAL, BOULDER VALLEY, CRAG, HIKERS TRACK, TRIALS AND TRENCHES, LEVERS WATER

■ EXCAVATION
– – COURSE OF VEIN
▨ SPOIL

**THE BACK STRINGS**
SCALE 0 10 20 30 40 YDS APPROX. 80

*Fig. 7    These open clefts are very dangerous! Early open
workings upon the veins, they have false floors with
very deep chasms below. DO NOT DESCEND INTO
THEM.*

disruptive effect on the veins are the Levers Water, and Great or
Kernal or Thriddle Cross-courses. Tracing these with any certainty
below ground is not easy.

It does appear that the cross-faulting may be subsequent to the
mineralisation period but in the absence of proper evidence they
might also really be contemporaneous. The Great Cross-course
appears to have thrown the Bonsor Vein well to the S.W. where it is
located on the other side under the name of Thriddle (sometimes
Fleming's) Vein. It must be pointed out though, that the
circumstance of a vein being cut off by a cross-fault does not admit

20

with certainty that it will be located, to the left or right, on the other side.

One other fault, lying to the south, but which does not appear to have had any effect upon the vein pattern is the Great Sulphur Lode which carries quantities of iron-pyrites.

Examples of faulting can be seen in a number of places including Fleming's Mine, Bouncy Mine, Deep Level, on the surface at Wetherlam Mine and in an adit which drains the Penny Rigg Quarry atTilberthwaite. The latter fault in fact also forms the northern end of the quarry. A 'text book' example of a 'heave' can be seen (below adit) in the side of South Shaft on South Vein located through Courteney's Cross-cut at Paddy End.

One of the best examples however (see Fig. 8) of the disruptive effect of a major cross-course (Levers Water Fault ?) is seen in the workings accessible from Hospital Level, also at Paddy End. The vein is cut off at Hospital Shaft and thrown 180 feet or more in a westerly direction where it resumes its regular NW-SE course. The vein appears to have been dragged (vein refraction) into the fault zone by those 'mind boggling' forces which tore the strata apart. The removal of the ore on Hospital/Grey Crag Level has left a very large open stope and part of this, in a badly shattered section, is seen to be striking NE-SW. A long exploratory tunnel, Brim Fell or Pudding Stone Cross-cut, has been driven along south-westerly and south along the major fault,

What is really needed, is a careful geological appraisal of the whole area. This should have been done below ground whilst the mine was in operation but indications are that geologists were not encouraged. The present state of the workings renders full investigation impossible and any intensive exploration of the backs is, it must be repeated, fraught with danger - in places bordering upon suicidal!

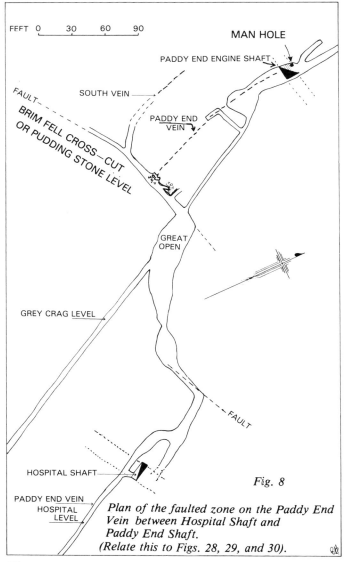

FEET 0   30   60   90

MAN HOLE

PADDY END ENGINE SHAFT

SOUTH VEIN

FAULT

BRIM FELL CROSS—CUT
OR PUDDING STONE LEVEL

PADDY END
VEIN

GREAT
OPEN

GREY CRAG LEVEL

FAULT

HOSPITAL SHAFT

PADDY END VEIN
HOSPITAL
LEVEL

*Fig. 8*

*Plan of the faulted zone on the Paddy End
Vein between Hospital Shaft and
Paddy End Shaft.
(Relate this to Figs. 28, 29, and 30).*

# 5. Field Guide for the visitor

## Route 1.
### Coniston Village to Red Dell & Thriddle Foot Workings; God's Blessing, Black Scar Workings and Sam Bottom.

In Coniston if a person turns up directly by the side of the Black Bull, and follows the road up, he will soon come to the fell gate beyond which the road becomes an unsurfaced cart-track .... cart-road if you wish. After a short distance the route traverses along the side of the deep gill or ravine of Church Beck and before the way was widened a few years ago, in connection with water-works, it was much narrower. Depending upon the weather the beck in the bottom can be but a gentle stream or, on the other hand, a rushing torrent. The Coniston Waterfalls, as they are now popularly known, might as a result be something of a disappointment but if the water is high then it will not be possible to get to the first of the tunnels, or levels, catalogued in this manual - Coniston Falls Level, we shall know it by.

Its entrance is hidden at the end of a natural cleft, at the extreme left-hand of the fall. Driven in for some 519 feet (see Fig. 8A) it runs for part of its length along a fault, which forms one wall of the tunnel; in doing so it provides an interesting cross-section (see insert in Fig. 8A). Finely divided haematite is seen to be associated with the fissure. The 'railway' in the tunnel seems to have consisted of boards along each side laid either on sleepers or directly onto the floor. Gaps between boards were frequently made good with slabs of slate. A strange affair indeed! The truck must have been a simple affair, with flangeless wheels, and low capacity. Such a waggon would have required both pushing and pulling. The waste from the driving (and the drilling was done by hand for the gunpowder charges ... possibly dynamite towards the end) was certainly 'lost' in the beck. The reason for putting in this tunnel is somewhat obscure; it would be absurd to consider driving an adit, or drainage level, all the way up to the copper mine. The working is quite safe although, it must be

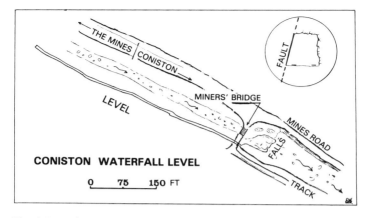

*Fig. 8A    The Plan shows that there is nothing complicated about Coniston Waterfall level. Geologically however (see insert) the tunnel is quite interesting.*

admitted, a trifle wet in the entrance.

Do not hasten off just yet, pause at the foot of the waterfall and look upstream. What a grand aspect it is, with Miners' Bridge surmounting the cascade. With a little imagination it might be possible to visualise the heavy cartloads of dressed ore, creaking their way across, and then down to the copper-house at the rail-head. After the railway was brought to Coniston the lake transport ceased and a way of life departed forever.

Alas! Already the writer is guilty of digression. This is a guide to the mines in the fells, as they are found contemporaneously. Yet, almost with every step one takes, one cannot avoid meeting the past. Throughout the book the reader might well, repeatedly, expect some explication which will be found, maddeningly perhaps, not to be forthcoming .... and the reason for this is simple, though apologies must surely be proffered. It is, that to spill-the-beans now would only detract from the forthcoming history!

Pass on therefore, up the mine road until, at the top of the rise, one is confronted suddenly and grandly, with Coppermines Valley. The white building ahead is the Coppermines House Youth Hostel but was formerly the mine office and manager's house. About it are the Bonsor Dressing Floors. We shall visit this site later. For now, just

24

over the rise take the right-hand fork in the road and follow up, past the collapsed bottom tunnel of the Blue Quarries (slate), and then up past the end of the row of miners' cottages, to where the quarry road is joined from the left by the Red Dell track. The latter was constructed for carting heavy mining machinery. If however, the quarry road is followed for a further 68 yards or so, another track will be seen branching off on the left. Climbing steeply, this passes through Hole Rake, skirts the old Moor Slate Quarries, and drops down into the wilderness above Tilberthwaite Gill.

Now head along the Red Dell track, and soon a large ice-smoothed rock outcrop will be seen on the right. Miner J. Mara chiselled his name into this in 1874 and again in 1877. The aerial ropeway, from the pillar on the top bank of Blue Quarry, down to the dressing floors below, passed just over about here and at some time it shed a load of stone - still lying on the track. Further on, the road passes over a short trial tunnel, and brings one eventually above the wheel-pit and winch house of the 18th century Bonsor East Shaft. It is easy to see that the wheel was fed from a sizeable water storage lagoon and that this in turn was fed by a leat, or race, from the beck where a wooden barrier diverted the water. Iron pins in the stream bed are still to be seen. The tail-race from the water-wheel was run off back down into the beck.

Bonsor East Shaft (see Fig. 9) is really a cleared and timbered way down through the open stope on the Bonsor Vein. It was decided not to extend it up to the surface, possibly to reduce the amount of water getting into the mine. Instead it was located in an underground chamber or shaft station and entry into this can scarcely be recommended.

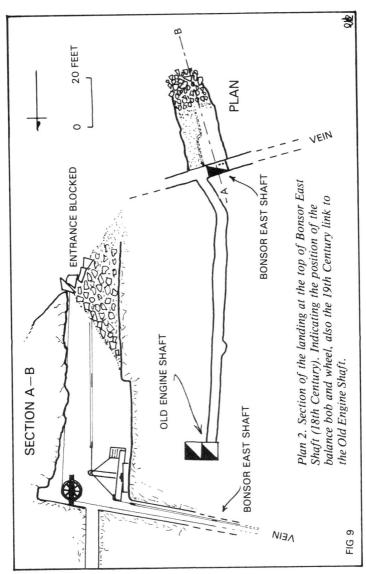

SECTION A—B

ENTRANCE BLOCKED

OLD ENGINE SHAFT

BONSOR EAST SHAFT

VEIN

PLAN

VEIN

BONSOR EAST SHAFT

BONSOR EAST SHAFT

0 20 FEET

*Plan 2. Section of the landing at the top of Bonsor East Shaft (18th Century). Indicating the position of the balance bob and wheel, also the 19th Century link to the Old Engine Shaft.*

FIG 9

In the 1800's when sinking the adjacent Old Engine Shaft, and before the Deep Level Cross-cut was completed, a link tunnel was driven from Bonsor East Shaft Station to Old Engine Shaft. Through this, and out to day, the debris from the sinking was brought and tipped near to the wheel-pit. This explains the presence of so much grey country rock amongst the brown vein waste.

Above the track, an iron-stained spoil heap is from a short cross-cut taken in to what is really the roof of the Bonsor Vein; and then along it for about 30 yards. A chain across the tunnel warns of a very deep hole in the floor, which is seen to be very thin, and this must have been a ventilation hole for the workings below. (Fig. 9A). From the entrance a pony track runs along the fell side only to lose itself in the vicinity of 'Old Man Old Wife Quarry', where, as well as a small open work, a level was taken in. This work was done many years ago by an old couple but their search for good slate 'metal' was fruitless for the rock there is fractured and stringed with quartz.

Heading towards the masonry tower, conspicuously ahead, note down on the left, alongside the lagoon and feed race to the East Shaft wheel, old surface workings along the outcrop of the Bonsor Vein. These were early 17th. Century German workings, which they knew as Low Works. In the crag above here, the steep natural cleft is Rough Gill, which, torrenting in wet weather, caused a considerable nuisance to the ancients - and to the 19th. Century adventurers. At the foot of the tower is the wheel pit which housed the large water wheel powering the Old Engine Shaft - raising the ore and working the pumps. What a grand sight it must have been when it was turning. Not far away is the tunnel, or 'bob-plat level', running to the top of the engine shaft itself. Chains have been fixed, as a safety measure, across the brink of the 15ft drop onto the balance-bob platform; at the far end of this is the 1,395 ft shaft. Formerly, with monotonous regularity, individuals fell down onto the ledge, sustaining thereby a variey of injuries and, of course, requiring rescue. Note that the heavy iron sheave wheel is still in place over the shaft. Observe also, the square timber hitches cut out in the tunnel side for a wooden walk-way long since vanished. This place is safe enough providing one does not pass the chains for a closer look! Do not throw stones into the shaft - there may be someone exploring in the mine below!

The slot in the floor of the tunnel housed a guide wheel or roller. Does Fig. 4 suggest what purpose it might have served? Note too the drill holes and grooves in the sides and roof. These were shot-holes, with gunpowder used for blasting. In the forebay of the tunnel, iron

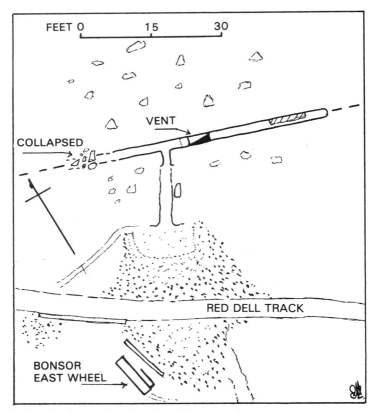

*Fig. 9A    Ventilation Level on Bonsor Vein.*

brackets let into the side, carried a gutter to direct dripping water away from the tunnel mouth.

The tail-race from the wheel-pit could be run off back into the beck, or across by a wooden flume, and along the race seen traversing along the opposite bank, and around Tongue Brow to the Paddy End dressing floors. Part of this race is tunnelled.

The water for the Old Engine Shaft wheel was carried by wooden sluice supported on the tower. It is possible to follow the feed race along to the Red Dell Beck, over which it was formerly ducted, and

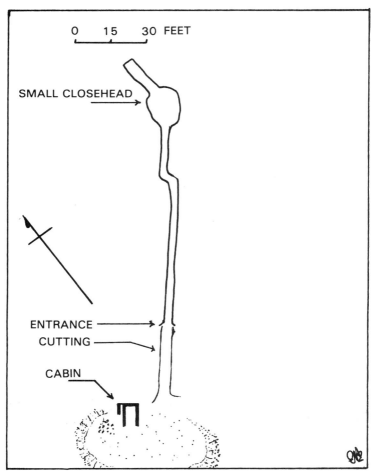

*Fig. 10    Lad Stones End Slate Level*

beyond it to the rail-race tunnel from the New Engine Shaft wheel-pit. Spoil from the Lad Stones End slate level (Fig. 10) encroaches onto the water-race indicating that at the time of driving (1910), the race was indeed abandoned.

From the cutting to the slate level mouth, a flood leat can be followed up diagonally to the bottom of Rough Gill. This was probably made in the early 1700's in an attempt to prevent floodwater from getting into the mine via the old outcrop workings below. Directly above the leat, roughly parallel, a cart track leads up to a small slate working in the crag, passing two tiny trials on the way up. Can you spot them? Look out for tell-tale shotholes.

Beyond the footbridge - over Red Dell Beck - deep and dangerous open stopes are to be seen, some of which are undoubtably ancient, and were called White or New Works by the 'Old Men'.

A few years ago an American youth fell into one of these stopes whilst leaping across; he was rescued but spent many months in hospital recovering from his serious injuries. He survived; the man who fell in 1978 did not - so take heed - DO NOT enter the fenced enclosure.

At the western end of the fissures is the 19th Century New Engine Shaft. The square hole was a ladder-way and the small round hole adjacent the winding rope/chain eye. Contiguous is the 18th Century Bonsor West Shaft. Note how the vein is shifted by faulting and it is cut off at the west end by the Great or Kernal Cross-course. The wheel-pit is seen to be well preserved, and from it, running steeply up the scree below Kernal Crag, is the Thriddle Incline.

(Study Figs. 11 and 12 in connection with this location.)


**Red Dell Ore Dressing Mill site -
A Question of Interpretation.**

The position of the old mill is a short distance along the valley bottom at Thriddle Foot (see Fig. 13). All such archaeological sites require translation into an apprehensible chronological sequence and none more so, perhaps, than this small locality for here we are presented with evidence of activity from the early 1600's right through to the opening years of the present century.

Certainly there was an active ore treatment mill here prior to 1620 for at that period, as a result of river silting, the mining company, and certain aggrieved tenants of land which was affected, were involved in a litigation. Findings were against the miners and damages were awarded accordingly.

No evidence of a wheel-pit remains, suggesting that this might have been a wooden structure. If of wood, i.e. wooden flume on stilts delivering to a wheel housed in a timber framework, it would be that much easier for its destruction by Parliamentarian forces during the Civil War. Do not forget that the mines were under the control of the 'Society of Mines Royal'.

The water-race collected from a stone dam upstream, and delivered as we can see, into a large raised masonry feed channel and lagoon. Could this be a pre-Civil War remnant? Or does it date, conceivably, from the late 17th Century when a group of Quakers were busy mining on the fells?

One positive clue is that Charles Roe, a Macclesfield silk industrialist turned mine adventurer, although having worked the Bonsor Vein for many years during the 1700's had, in 1783, a large quantity of 'small ore', presumably low grade stuff, which had been obtained at the 'beginning of the work' but which could not be weighed until 'stamped or broken by an engine and washed'. They were going to erect one with all speed but were 'distressed for some sycamore wood for the water wheel'. This was obtained and doubtless the stamping machine was set up, but, was Charles Roe's mill on this site? Certainly he worked the Bonsor Vein, (well below the 'old mens' workings), using wheels at his Bonsor East and West Shafts. Was his ore brought up here to Thriddle Foot to process? Did he have more than one mill? An early print published in 1820, shows a copper mill at Coniston. Unfortunately, whilst this is quite probably Roe's Mill, artistic licence in re-positioning mountains, combines to make site identification difficult. It may well be Thriddle Foot Mill which would have been idle at that time.

To confuse matters a little more, Fleming's Level was driven in the 1820's from here; its rails clearly spanned the lagoon and the spoil heap is easily recognisable. A reception floor was provided for ore and this is still to be seen. The writer believes that the ore, after a preliminary cobbing was simply carted down to the dressing floors below Bonsor which were at that time under construction.

Thriddle Incline was built during the same period, to serve the Thriddle or Bouncy Shaft which was being sunk down the vein to form part of what became known as Fleming's Mine. This shaft was at first powered by the old Bonsor West Shaft wheel, which was also named Millican's Wheel after the attendant of that name who met with a fearful end in its pit as a result of being careless whilst oiling the machine.

Later, when the large wheels for the Old and New Engine Shafts were commissioned - replacing the Bonsor East and West wheels, the Red

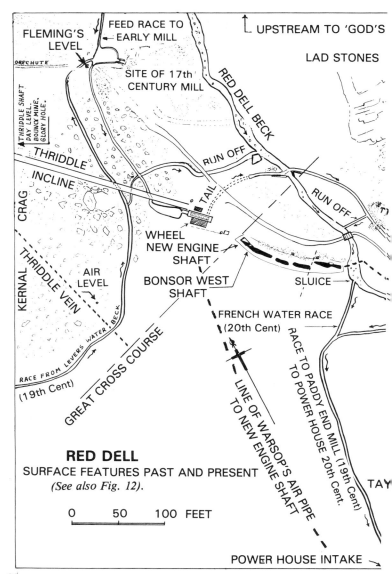

UPSTREAM TO 'GOD'S LAD STONES

FLEMING'S LEVEL

FEED RACE TO EARLY MILL

ORECHUTE

SITE OF 17th CENTURY MILL

RED DELL BECK

THRIDDLE SHAFT, DAY LEVEL, BOUNCY MINE, GLORY HOLE.

THRIDDLE INCLINE

RUN OFF

TAIL

RUN OFF

CRAG

THRIDDLE VEIN

KERNAL

AIR LEVEL

WHEEL NEW ENGINE SHAFT

BONSOR WEST SHAFT

SLUICE

RACE FROM LEVERS WATER BECK

GREAT CROSS COURSE

(19th Cent)

FRENCH WATER RACE (20th Cent)

RACE TO PADDY END MILL (19th Cent) TO POWER HOUSE 20th Cent.

LINE OF WARSOP'S AIR PIPE TO NEW ENGINE SHAFT

**RED DELL**

SURFACE FEATURES PAST AND PRESENT
*(See also Fig. 12).*

0      50      100  FEET

TAY

POWER HOUSE INTAKE

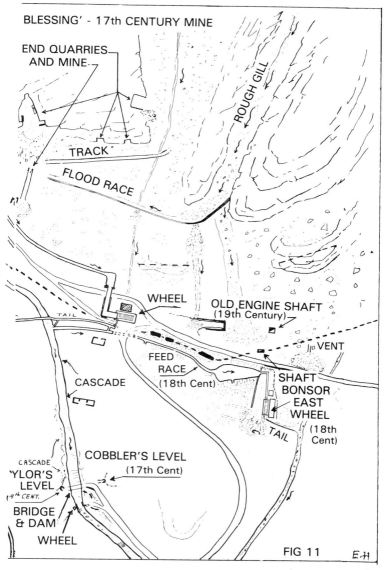

BLESSING' - 17th CENTURY MINE

END QUARRIES AND MINE

TRACK

FLOOD RACE

ROUGH GILL

WHEEL

TAIL

OLD ENGINE SHAFT
(19th Century)

VENT

FEED RACE
(18th Cent)

SHAFT
BONSOR
EAST
WHEEL
(18th Cent)

TAIL

CASCADE

CASCADE

COBBLER'S LEVEL
(17th Cent)

'YLOR'S LEVEL
19th CENT.

BRIDGE & DAM

WHEEL

FIG 11

E.H

33

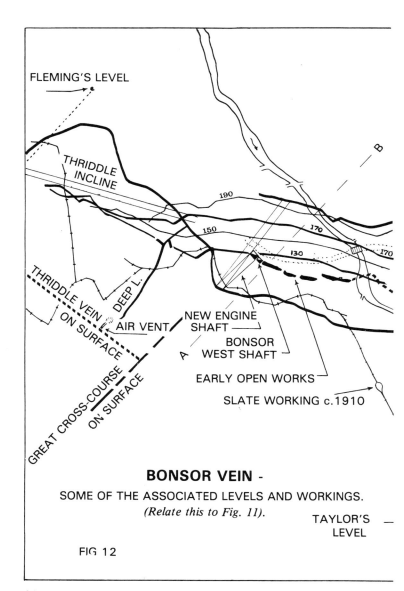

FLEMING'S LEVEL

THRIDDLE INCLINE

190

150

170

130

170

THRIDDLE VEIN ON SURFACE

DEEP L.

GREAT CROSS-COURSE ON SURFACE

AIR VENT

A

NEW ENGINE SHAFT

BONSOR WEST SHAFT

EARLY OPEN WORKS

SLATE WORKING c.1910

B

## BONSOR VEIN -

SOME OF THE ASSOCIATED LEVELS AND WORKINGS.
*(Relate this to Fig. 11).*

TAYLOR'S LEVEL

FIG 12

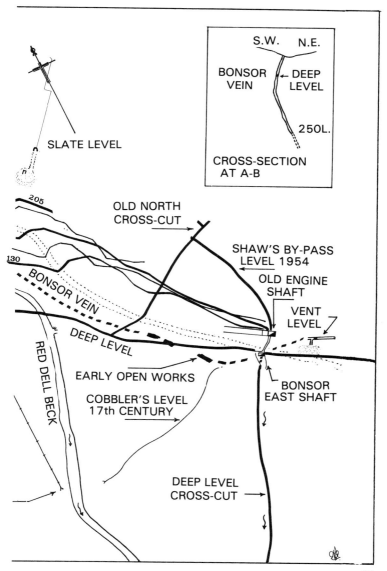

S.W.　N.E.

BONSOR VEIN ← DEEP LEVEL

250L.

CROSS-SECTION AT A-B

SLATE LEVEL

205

OLD NORTH CROSS-CUT

SHAW'S BY-PASS LEVEL 1954

OLD ENGINE SHAFT

130

BONSOR VEIN

VENT LEVEL

DEEP LEVEL

RED DELL BECK

EARLY OPEN WORKS

BONSOR EAST SHAFT

COBBLER'S LEVEL 17th CENTURY

DEEP LEVEL CROSS-CUT →

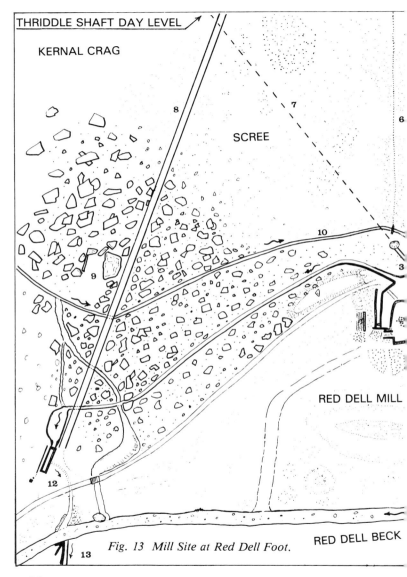

THRIDDLE SHAFT DAY LEVEL

KERNAL CRAG

SCREE

RED DELL MILL

RED DELL BECK

*Fig. 13  Mill Site at Red Dell Foot.*

36

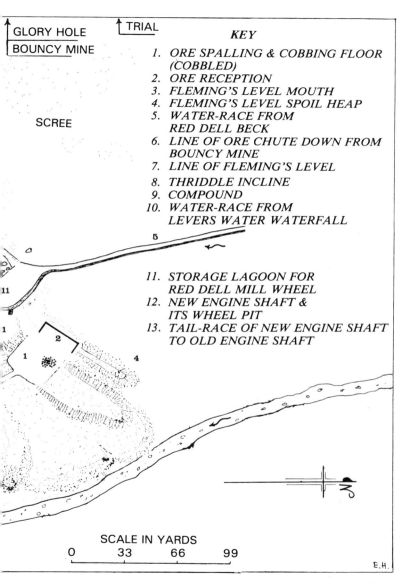

GLORY HOLE
BOUNCY MINE

↑ TRIAL

**KEY**

1. ORE SPALLING & COBBING FLOOR (COBBLED)
2. ORE RECEPTION
3. FLEMING'S LEVEL MOUTH
4. FLEMING'S LEVEL SPOIL HEAP
5. WATER-RACE FROM RED DELL BECK
6. LINE OF ORE CHUTE DOWN FROM BOUNCY MINE
7. LINE OF FLEMING'S LEVEL
8. THRIDDLE INCLINE
9. COMPOUND
10. WATER-RACE FROM LEVERS WATER WATERFALL

SCREE

11. STORAGE LAGOON FOR RED DELL MILL WHEEL
12. NEW ENGINE SHAFT & ITS WHEEL PIT
13. TAIL-RACE OF NEW ENGINE SHAFT TO OLD ENGINE SHAFT

SCALE IN YARDS

0    33    66    99

E.H.

Dell Beck was found inadequate in dry weather, and a new race was brought all the way from Levers Water Beck, along below Kernal Crag, passing under the incline and running along to discharge into the lagoon.

Well above the mill site, below the gaping hole in Thriddle Scar and not too far from the top of the incline, is Bouncy Mine put in during 1907. Ore was chuted down (can you spot the line of the chute), and taken away by cart. Thus we have a little more superimposition - the low wall which supported the chute partly obstructs the Levers Water Beck race, just above the lagoon.

By following the beck upstream, a small cascade will be arrived at and here, hidden in the bank, is a tiny ancient tunnel which terminates after a few feet in a flooded, wood-lined, sump.

**Fleming's Mine** (*see sketch plan Fig. 14*)

A wedged bottomless steel drum slopes steeply down into the wet lower end of Fleming's Level. The cross-cut, driven south-westerly at about right angles to the vein, is in sound rock but the unwary may be subjected to a ducking in a sump at the first junction where a trial has been made to the left and right along a quartz string. The vein was reached after 420 feet of driving and it is seen to be steeply inclined - which fact caused John Barrett a fair amount of concern whilst the level was being driven in the 1820's .... but that is another story.

The left hand branch runs along the vein for some 240 feet to where it is cut off by a fault - most likely the Great Cross-course. Here a ventilation raise was put up to the surface (see in Index: Fleming's Mine Ventilation Shaft.) This was much needed in the period preceeding connection with the workings rising from Taylor's Level below. Over much of the length the floor is seen to be taken out and back-filled - indeed it is possible that waste was trammed back in for this purpose. A pumping and winding sump at the cross-cut junction no longer exists but of course it would have been rendered obsolete when connection was made with Taylor's workings. The acute dip of the lode creates instability of the hanging wall in places. Indeed progress is soon halted (after about 70 feet along the right hand branch) by a section of floor which has been dragged down by a large flake detaching from the side - probably hastened by dry-rot. At the end of the pit the level is seen to continue. At the far lower end an access tube leads into a continuation of the vein for here a fault has

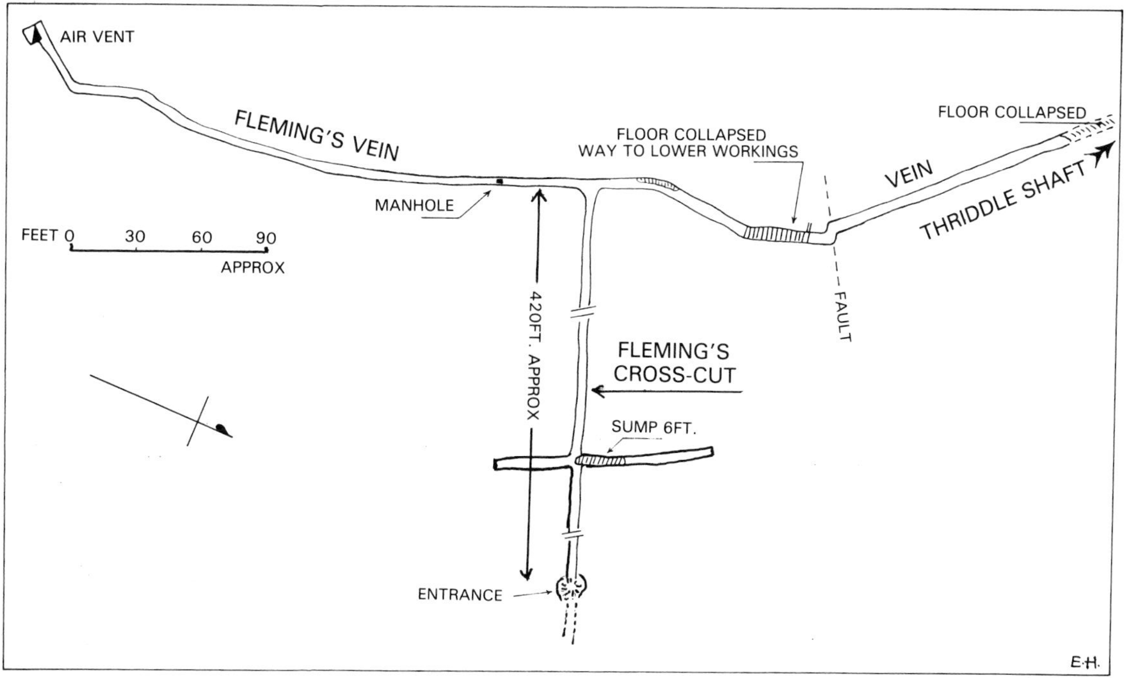

Fig. 14   Sketch Plan of Fleming's Level.

FLOOR COLLAPSED

THRIDDLE SHAFT

VEIN

FAULT

FLOOR COLLAPSED
WAY TO LOWER WORKINGS

FLEMING'S CROSS-CUT

SUMP 6FT.

420FT. APPROX

ENTRANCE

MANHOLE

FLEMING'S VEIN

AIR VENT

FEET 0    30    60    90
APPROX

E.H.

shifted it to the left. In this further extension good examples of the timberman's art are to be seen; an ore chute in the vein itself, and in an electron ladder pitch the vein is seen to narrow quite remarkably. It is not proposed to continue this description to the point where it is too difficult to be interpreted by the average reader. The continuation of Fleming's Level, on the other side of the hole, was entered by explorers using a scaling pole and electron ladder. Hopes were raised of reaching the 'station' where Thriddle Shaft passed down through. Alas, about after about 42 yards decaying floor timbers have given way and the length of the collapse with the great hole beneath precludes further progress without risk. The shaft is about 120 feet ahead of this position and 'tin cans' dropped down from above, at a pre-arranged time, clattered ahead quite distinctly. Much of the woodwork in here is not to be trusted - damp conditions have in  places been favourable for the spread of dry-rot and the wood is now 156 years old. *Investigation of this interesting old working cannot be recommended to any group except those properly equipped and experienced.*


God's Blessing

Continue up the valley, past the washing dam and sheep fold, and the remains of small stone compounds - possibly miners' or travellers' sheds - may be recognised. At about an altitude of 1,725 feet, (100 yards above the convergence of a side stream from the right) one arrives at the little known God's Blessing Mine. A tiny hand-made plateau on the right bank was certainly for the preparation and loading into leather or basket saddle bags of ore won from the level in the opposite bank. This is a hand wrought coffin shaped tunnel, modified in the early 1900's by hand drilled holes and dynamite. The tunnel cuts through two veins, but there is scarcely any mineralisation to be seen, though it was once a very hopeful prospect of the early miners. The entrance is partly blocked, there is water in the tunnel, and if care is taken not to fall into the flooded sump then it is quite safe to explore. (see Fig. 15).

About 44 yards upstream, on the same side, are inundated workings on the outcrop of the vein, though again with poor showings of copper. There may be a blocked level in the other bank and 50 yards to the east, a sump or shaft is sunk upon the vein. God's Blessing Vein, indeed, can be traced eastwards up Lower Hows (part of Wetherlam), across the top and down Hen Crag into the bottom of

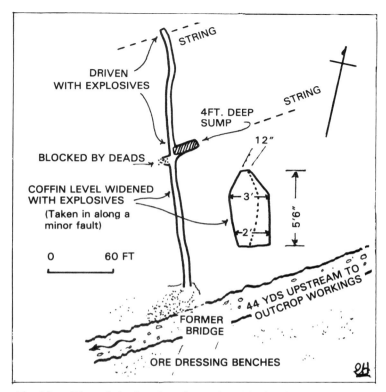

*Fig. 15    Plan of the Level at the ancient 'Gods Blessing Mine' in Red Dell.*

upper Tilberthwaite - bearing generally in the direction of Tilberthwaite Mine of which it may be a continuation of the North Lode there.

From God's Blessing the vein may also be seen coursing more-or-less south-westerly, up and over Low Wether Crag and down to near Sam Bottom where there is a small working on this lode.

From God's Blessing it is but a short distance up valley to where one can look down into upper Greenburn. The Greenburn Mine is described later in the book.

41

*To continue the present trip we must retrace our steps back down to the New Engine Shaft wheel.)*

From New Engine Shaft ascend the Thriddle Incline which will bring the reader to the mouth of the Thriddle or Bouncy Shaft Balance-bob Level. The 42 yards long tunnel is safe enough but beware of falling onto the bob platform - chains have not been fixed yet. Of particular interest is the discovery of the old wooden bob still in site though minus its bishop's head, nose, and axle/bearing castings (shown in Fig. 5). The deep shaft is at the far end, dropping down for hundreds of feet, intersecting Fleming's Mine and Level, and ending well below Deep Level far below. The small iron pivot in the tunnel mouth changed the direction of the engine house-to-shaft signalling wire. There was also a much larger pivot here for changing the angle of the pump-rods. Examination will reveal the square timber hitches in the sides. There would also have been a sheave wheel here as well for the winding chain or wire rope but, unlike the example of the Old Engine Shaft, the wheel here and at the shaft top is missing - either taken for scrap or used elsewhere in the mine. The entrance must have appeared rather cluttered (see Fig. 16) but ore was not brought out of the entrance. Winding in this shaft was up to Fleming's Level and then, as the mine deepened, up to Deep Level and the same thing applied to the water. Any water collecting in the shaft as it was sunk down to the workings on Fleming's Level would have been lifted out by kibble. The writer supposes that it is just possible that any ore got during the early sinking might have been pack-horsed down to the mill. On the other hand it could very well have been piled at the entrance and dropped down the shaft when connection was made with the workings on the Fleming's Level. It would then have been brought out of Fleming's Level mouth.

Not far above here is the buried entrance to Bouncy Mine. Put in in 1907, the cross-cut runs in for about 55 feet to intersect the vein which is also cut off here by a cross-fault. A drive has been taken along the vein, to the right, for some 145 feet laying open a quantity of low grade ore which was never worked. Ore brought out from this development was, as mentioned earlier, chuted down from the entrance to some sort of cart loading arrangement at the bottom.

In Thriddle Scar above here are two trials on the same vein which is exposed quite clearly. The nearest and largest is in the form of a cavern some 44 ft. long by 11 ft. wide and 18 ft. high. Studying Fig. 17 it will be seen that the vein is split in here by a barren 'rider' or 'horse'. The working is safe enough save that at one point a raise was put up from Bouncy Mine below and the floor rubble sits upon timbers across this. Descent into Bouncy Mine (which is not at all

42

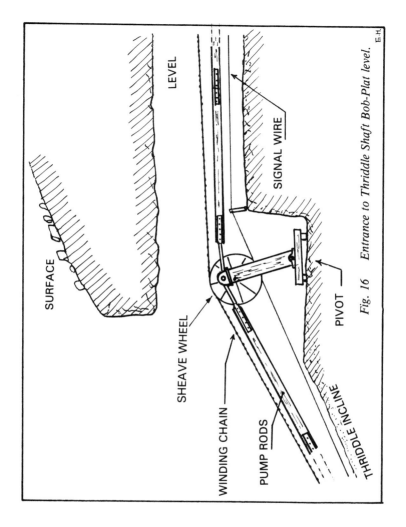

LEVEL

SIGNAL WIRE

SURFACE

PIVOT

SHEAVE WHEEL

WINDING CHAIN

PUMP RODS

THRIDDLE INCLINE

E.H.

*Fig. 16    Entrance to Thriddle Shaft Bob-Plat level.*

43

dangerous) revealed the place exactly as it was abandoned. The relationship between these two workings is shown in Fig. 17. Twenty-five yards along the cliff is the other, similar but smaller, trial - this with a flooded sump. Both are of some age but the largest, known to the workmen as 'Glory Hole', has been enlarged from time to time …. in 1907, for example, with explosive. Each is marked 'Level' on the map.

From Glory Hole a pony track leads up onto the top and thence by cart-road, now well grassed over, to link with the Paddy End/Levers Water Track a little below the Levers Water Dam spillway. The vein however may be traced from the top of the scar, above Glory Hole, along and over to the south-east margin of the tarn (Levers Water). Its strike is indicated by tiny trials upon it and there are also two prospecting trenches (dug maybe several hundred years ago) one of which is 36 feet and the longest 165 feet in length. As the tarn is neared the vein has been too deeply buried, beneath rocky ground, to explore easily by pits or trenches. By the water's edge however, there is one or more diggings: perhaps one might have been a short tunnel.

The vein passes below the tarn and is next seen outcropping on the steep fell-side between Great and Little How Crags where it appears from a distance as a foaming cascade. The white 'foam' however, is milky quartz. Here at an altitude of about 2,200 feet the ancients worked an open-cut and put in one or more levels. One is still open and has been extended to some 201 feet in more recent times with the aid of dynamite. It is perfectly safe, and it will be seen that its end has been taken along the vein, which is very poor really. The mine is shown on the map as 'Black Scar Working'.

Above the knoll, beyond the north-western margin of the tarn, and below the crag known as 'The Prison', are the remains of a compound and sheds and this is about 300 yards from the last mentioned level. Probably used as a sheep fold in years past, the writer likes to link it with the mines - perhaps as a rude habitation, possibly with a small smithy. Above it, in the lower part of the ruckle of boulders below The Prison, is a curious circular masonry structure more than likely a fox trap and as such quite a rare Lakeland feature. Some 5 or 6 feet high and strongly built with walls 3 feet thick at the top, it has an internal diameter of 9 feet with no doors or windows. In amongst the great spill of rocks and boulders above here, numerous cavities under large slabs, have been partly walled up forming small shelters  (?). It has been put forward that all this walling - and there's a lot of it - was to 'keep foxes out'. Yet this seems unlikely for there are literally thousands of places a fox could

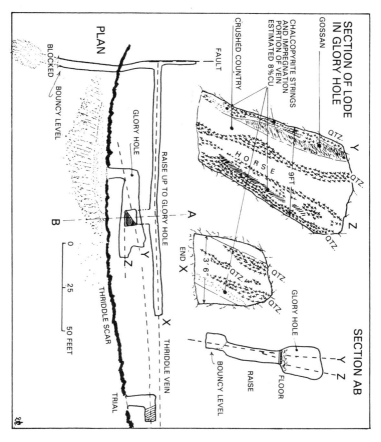

Fig. 17    Plan and section of 'Glory Hole' in Thriddle Scar and
Bouncy Mine below.

hide. A large cleft in the cliff above here can be entered - a stone slab made a convenient seat inside. Why is this spot named The Prison? Is there some cryptic secret concerning this place lost in the mists of time?

Continue up Levers Water Hause, past The Prison, following Swirl Hause Beck past Sam Bottom to arrive at GR.2785.0024 where there is a trial upon a strong quartz vein. There may have been a tunnel here as well as the open-cut. Note remains of small cabin. Keen eyes may have spotted fragments of aircraft wreckage lying around. Unfortunately, this is steadily disappearing.

The vein may be seen streaking westwards up and over the tops of Swirl Band - behind The Prison. Eastwards, it can be traced easily to a small cave or trial, and up and over the top of Low Wether Crag and it can then be seen to be God's Blessing Vein - crossing Red Dell.

The hiker's track (along this, the eastern side of the valley) can be followed up and over into the head of Greenburn Valley where there is much wreckage from yet another sad World War II air-crash.

*Route 2*
## Coniston Mine/Bonsor Dressing Floors, Deep Adit Level, Cobblers and Taylor's Level.

Instead of turning off up the Blue Quarry track (see Route 1) continue straight on, past Irish Row, in the direction of the Youth Hostel. Far ahead a large diameter pipeline can be seen running down the fellside. This delivered high pressure water to a pelton-wheel which latterly powered a compressor delivering air to slate quarries in the vicinity. The building, which is now in a bad state, was originally the mine sawmill and the wheel-pit at one side is in splendid condition. It was also the generating station and electro-precipitation house of the French 'Coniston Electrolytic Copper Company' of First World War times.

The complex of terraces, walls and ruined buildings form the Bonsor Dressing Floors. Below the mine office was the Low Mill, where final washing of the ore was carried out, whilst behind the building was the Upper Mill where the run-of-mine ore was given its primary treatment. In the main the site owes its appearance to the 19th Century (dating from 1832, although there may have been an earlier mill hereabouts) but it has been modified by the French concern. Slate has been dressed on the site too, the material being lowered to here from the top of the Blue Quarries, by aerial ropeway.

By studying Figs. 18 and 19 one is able to visualise to some degree the extent of activities at these mills where almost 200 persons were employed in the heyday of the mine. Fig. 20 shows how much altered things had become by 1914.

To locate the masonry arched entrance to Deep Adit Level - from out of which most of the ore (and rock waste) was brought in horse (Galloway) drawn mine wagons - follow Red Dell beck up past the ruined compressor house when the tunnel mouth will come into view in the right hand bank. Although horses were used in almost all the levels this one was popularly the 'Horse Level'.

Deep Level (as we shall call it) (Fig. 21) was the lowest drainage level that could, with any economy, be driven. It also had to be in a position convenient for the intended dressing mill site. Taking years to drive, the tunnel connects the engine shafts on the Bonsor Vein, including Thriddle Shaft, follows the Great Cross-course along which it was close timbered, to link up with the shafts and workings at Paddy End.

*Fig. 18    Bonsor Upper Mill.*

The rock passage is safe enough as far as its intersection with the Bonsor Vein. See Fig. 22. From here though, carelessness or fooling around can place the intruder in jeopardy.

Just before the junction a thin copper vein is cut by the level and it can be seen gleaming dully on the left. Please do not bash it with your hammers - leave it for others to see. The iron pipe protruding from the floor ahead is, in fact, projecting from the Bonsor East Shaft, so take care at this point! It is the rising-main and runs down the shaft into the Old Engine Shaft, where they converge, and down to the pumping sump on the 170 fathom level. How many feet down is that below where you are standing?

Fig. 22 shows that a short distance ahead is the Old Engine Shaft. The ladders, used by the miners in the climbing compartment, may be seen in the shimmering green depths.

On the Bonsor Vein the easterly and westerly branches of the Deep

E.H.
1978

Level are blocked by dangerous falls of rock.

From Deep Level mouth, follow the old cart-track up-stream and after 29 yards notice the boulder blasted during widening operations. Dating back to the early 1600's, this was originally a pony or pack-horse route and indeed, the old path may even have been a long established route pre-dating the mining. Some 70 yards up from the Deep Level, the track is seen to be blasted out of a sloping bench of rock, but just above, carved from the solid mass, the original pony-track is observable. There is even a tiny drain or gutter cut across it at its lower end. A short distance further from here, a right fork climbs up to the wheel-pit of the Bonsor East Shaft and continues to Red Dell Foot. Probably the path was widened by Charles Roe around 1760. By following the lower track however, one arrives almost at the entrance of Cobblers Level (Fig. 23) which penetrates north-easterly to cut the Bonsor Lode. It has been taken in along a minor fault or

49

*Fig. 19    Bonsor Low Mill.*

joint and follows its meanderings for about 82 yards to a junction, where, 5 feet from the end, a left-hand branch is taken off to cut the vein - though unfortunately the old stope is choked by deads. Innumerable tool marks leave no doubt that the tunnel was entirely driven by hand, and likely dates back to the early 17th Century. Numerous small hitches cut into the walls about a foot from the roof, suggest stemples of wood were placed across, these supporting a partition or ceiling leaving a void. Fire-setting was probably used in the driving and smoke would be carried away to the entrance by this means. By today's standards how painfully slow this 'stollen' must have inched ahead! The miners were quite right in taking advantage of the joint as a plane of weakness to assist them, but it is surprising that they did not appreciate that as they neared the vein the joint went off-course and began to run parallel. This resulted in them doing much more work than was necessary. Perhaps the surveyor, if there was one, received a 'rocket' for his error!

Cobblers Level is a good example of a 'coffin level'. These were cut out narrow at the top, wider for the shoulders and tapering towards the base. Originally driven to drain the deepening Low Work, it would also have been used to bring out ore in leather shoulder bags

The left-hand branch was driven steeply up to connect with the bottom of the sinking workings which were to be drained. Close study has revealed that at some later date (almost certainly in Charles Roes's time), the tunnel was widened at the base.

Furthermore the branch has had its floor lowered leaving it over 12 feet in height where it enters the vein. Possibly a foot or more of the floor was taken out over the remainder of the tunnel, and if the short 'virgin' length at the end can be regarded as standard, then the original tunnel was about 5 feet 6 inches high whereas it is now much higher.

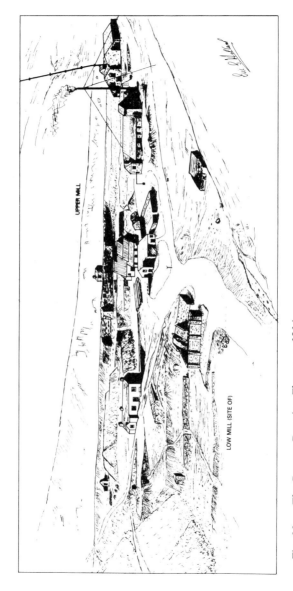

*Fig. 20    The Bonsor Dressing Floors - c. 1914.*

*Fig 21     Deep Adit Level Entrance.*

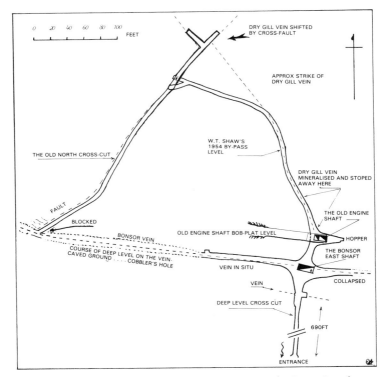

*Fig. 22    Plan showing accessible workings on the Deep Level at Bonsor. (Bonsor East Shaft 'Bob-Plat' Level omitted for clarity).*

54

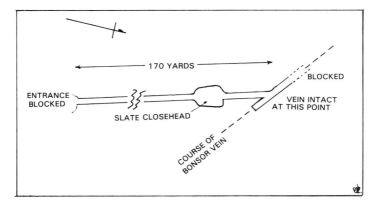

*Fig. 24    Sketch Plan of Taylor's Level showing intersection with Bonsor Vein and the small slate working.*

Several years ago the writer unblocked Taylor's and waded up the level to a slate closehead (1910) where a fine iron jumper drill was found. This slate band is the same one on which Lad Stones End Quarry was opened. After passing this point, the tunnel cut the Bonsor vein, but although a good section of the lode is to be seen in the roof, the main stope was blocked with timber, smashed ladders, rock, soil etc. through which the ventilation currents puffed and roared like distant surf.

If the bed of the beck be followed up, from the rock across which the pack-horse trail is carved, to the first cascade, a 3 inch vein carrying copper, lead, zinc and pyrite is seen in the right-hand wall. A trial, probably missed as you walked the track, is just above here and is likely of some antiquity.

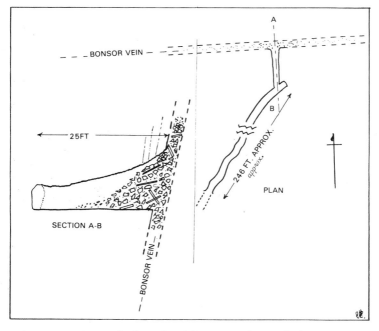

*Fig. 23  Section and Plan of Cobbler's Level, a 17th Century
Coffin Level.*

Taylor's Level (Fig. 24) lies across the other side of the beck but the
entrance is usually covered by debris washed down the fell-side. It is
located just below two shot-hole grooves in the rock, just a little to
the left of the cascade. Formerly our cart-track crossed the beck at
the foot of the cascade by means of a bridge, and ran to the entrance.
Note the iron holding-down pins set into the rock hereabouts.

Just a little downwards from Taylor's Level a square pit suggests a
waterwheel in the stream bed, with a pit providing clearance for a
pumping or balance-bob weight box. This would have been for a
pump in the workings below Taylor's prior to connection with those
raising from Deep Level below. There would have been a need for
such a pump and it is quite possible that the wheel was also equipped
with a winch to perform temporary internal winding.  (Fig. 25)

Fig. 25    *Taylor's Level. Reconstruction of the Pumping*
          *Apparatus. c. 1840*

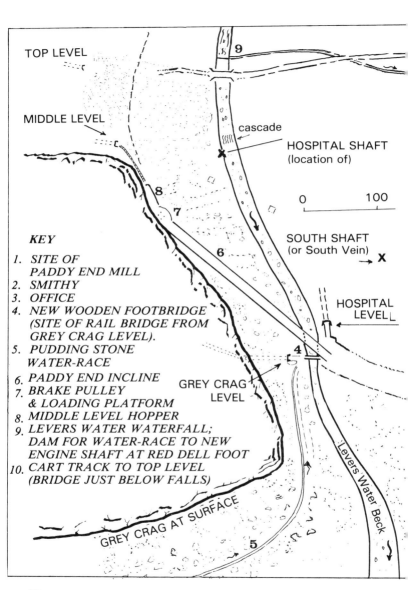

TOP LEVEL

MIDDLE LEVEL

cascade

HOSPITAL SHAFT
(location of)

SOUTH SHAFT
(or South Vein)

HOSPITAL
LEVEL

GREY CRAG
LEVEL

*KEY*

1. *SITE OF
   PADDY END MILL*
2. *SMITHY*
3. *OFFICE*
4. *NEW WOODEN FOOTBRIDGE
   (SITE OF RAIL BRIDGE FROM
   GREY CRAG LEVEL).*
5. *PUDDING STONE
   WATER-RACE*
6. *PADDY END INCLINE*
7. *BRAKE PULLEY
   & LOADING PLATFORM*
8. *MIDDLE LEVEL HOPPER*
9. *LEVERS WATER WATERFALL;
   DAM FOR WATER-RACE TO NEW
   ENGINE SHAFT AT RED DELL FOOT*
10. *CART TRACK TO TOP LEVEL
    (BRIDGE JUST BELOW FALLS)*

GREY CRAG AT SURFACE

Levers Water Beck

0          100

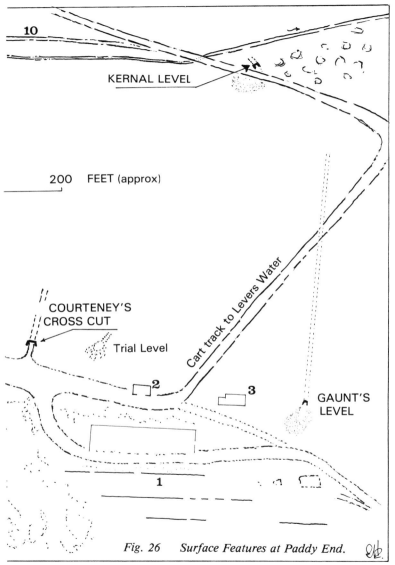

**10**

KERNAL LEVEL

200 FEET (approx)

COURTENEY'S CROSS CUT

Trial Level

Cart track to Levers Water

2

3

GAUNT'S LEVEL

1

*Fig. 26    Surface Features at Paddy End.*

## Route 3
## Bonsor Dressing Floors to Paddy End, Levers Water and the Back Strings, and Brim Fell Workings.
*(Study Fig. 26 first)*

Follow the mine road past Coppermines House, the Youth Hostel, and, just prior to commencing the climb up to Paddy End note on the right the old gunpowder house with a portion of its blast wall still intact. As one tops the short climb the Paddy End Dressing Floors, overshadowed by Grey Crag, come suddenly into view and dominating this scene is the sombre mass of Brimfell with Grey Crag dwarfed below it. The immediate foreground was formerly the terraced slime disposal area for the mill. The siting of a large, partly buried, concrete water treatment tank has however, eliminated the few features which had survived. By continuing up the track to the floors the ruined office and the smiths' shop are just above and in the latter remains of the hearth and wooden anvil stump are still to be seen. While following the track along towards the Grey Crag a tunnel will be passed. This is Courteney's Cross-cut to the South Vein. *Great care must be taken in here!* The right hand branch has a deep flooded sump in the floor and beyond that the roof is unsafe. The left hand branch runs into the deep South Shaft at which point the floor of the level is planked over. Although this wood was only put in in the 1950's during an investigation by McKechnie Bros. Ltd., it is not as strong or resistant to decay as the oak and sycamore of the old days. It was down through the tiny square trapdoor that a dog named Guinness fell and which was rescued, miraculously alive, after a sojourn of 27 days in the dark. It had fallen about 180 feet. The vein is faulted here and a text-book example of a heave is seen in the side of the shaft some 40 feet below. The blocked top of the South Shaft can be located on the hillside above.

A little distance from Courteney's Cross-cut is Paddy End Beck where is the mouth of Hospital Level and on the opposite bank, by the huge rock, the collapsed entrance to Grey Crag Level - one of the earlier important undertakings of the 19th Century. The mouths of these two levels are illustrated in the reconstruction, Fig. 31.

Hospital Level gives access to the ramification of workings on Grey Crag Level, (see Figs. 8, 28 and 29) but exploration is not without accompanying hazard and once more the writer advises that there is *no recommendation* for any but those experienced and equipped to investigate. Figure 28 shows that the drive soon forks and the right-hand branch is, in fact, quite safe, if a little wet. It terminates where

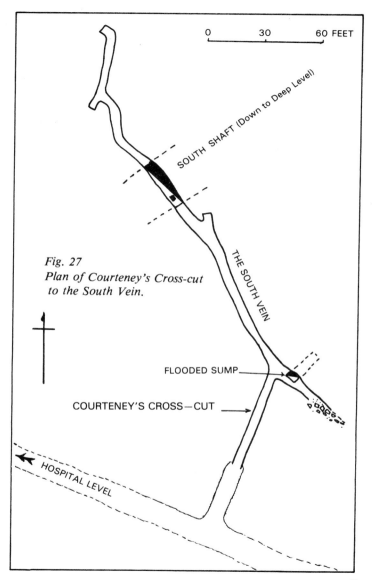

0   30   60 FEET

SOUTH SHAFT (Down to Deep Level)

THE SOUTH VEIN

Fig. 27
Plan of Courteney's Cross-cut
to the South Vein.

FLOODED SUMP

COURTENEY'S CROSS—CUT →

HOSPITAL LEVEL

61

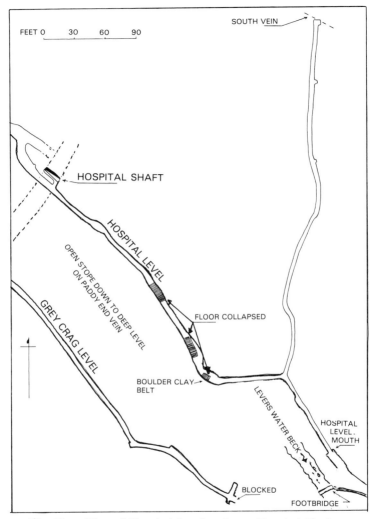

SOUTH VEIN

FEET 0    30    60    90

HOSPITAL SHAFT

HOSPITAL LEVEL

OPEN STOPE DOWN TO DEEP LEVEL ON PADDY END VEIN

GREY CRAG LEVEL

FLOOR COLLAPSED

BOULDER CLAY BELT

LEVERS WATER BECK

HOSPITAL LEVEL. MOUTH

BLOCKED

FOOTBRIDGE

*Fig. 28    Plan of Hospital Level as far as Hospital Shaft.
(relate this to Figs. 8, 29, 30).*

a thin copper-bearing string is cut - probably South Vein. The left-hand passage leads directly into the upper limits of the Paddy End Vein reached after negotiating a rather hair-raising section through boulder clay - debris, likely, from the last ice age. Directly following this the floor will seem to have been mined away and the resulting pit needs circumnavigating with due respect. Ahead in the level, floor timbers are giving way, yielding glimpses of the abysmal drop down through the old stopes to the rock strewn bottom. In an opening to the right, Hospital Shaft descends to where fallen matter prevents entry to Deep Level some 230 feet below Hospital Level. Under this debris is a whitewashed 'engine room' used for hoisting from the bottoms, to Deep Level hoppers. The shaft now resembles a part of the stope itself with very few timbers still in position. This was one of the last major works on the mine. It continues, up from Hospital Level, to surface but has been long covered by loose scree.

After passing the shaft, a climb up gives into a faulted and crushed zone, which soon leads into a stope of considerable dimensions and which is at variance with the general strike of Paddy End Vein. This section is given some attention in the chapter 'Geological Outline' and is illustrated in Fig. 8. Almost at the end of this great stope Grey Crag Level will be seen to come in at an acute angle and this may be waded down to its choked mouth. At this, the western extremity of the stope, a dry tunnel runs off to the south-west along a major fault. This is a prospecting tunnel and is known as 'Pudding Stone Level' or 'Brimfell Cross-cut'; it was driven to try the fault and to seek for and investigate the distant Brim Fell Vein. Entering, one is soon forced to crawl past a run-in which is probably from a working on the Paddy End Vein, (study Fig. 8) then past a deep and high open stope on South Vein (a different one!), and after about 900 feet progress is stopped by a blockage of fine fault-stuff and water. There have been one or two probes just here but the tunnel carries on for some 630 feet further along this, or another. fault. Clearing this could be a good project but the loose nature of the ground suggests similar blockages ahead.

Near the mouth of this long cross-cut, a low tunnel will be observed running off to the north-west and this is the continuance of Grey Crag Level. It leads into an engine-room in which was housed one of those horse powered winding machines known as a 'gin' which in this case was used for hoisting during the early period of the Paddy End Engine Shaft. During its sinking, material was lifted up to Grey Crag Level, but this duty was eventually taken over by mechanical means.

The Paddy End Shaft is just ahead and you are once again in the vein of the name. The shaft climbs up from below Deep Level,

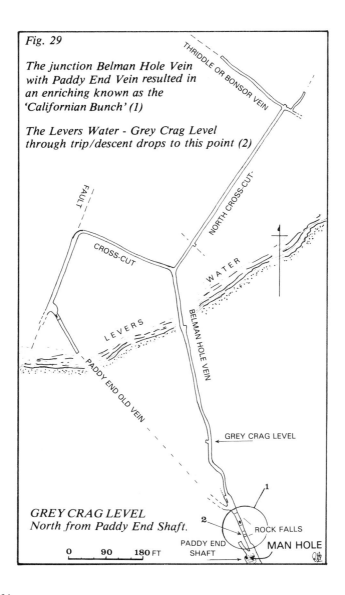

Fig. 29

The junction Belman Hole Vein with Paddy End Vein resulted in an enriching known as the 'Californian Bunch' (1)

The Levers Water - Grey Crag Level through trip/descent drops to this point (2)

THRIDDLE OR BONSOR VEIN

NORTH CROSS-CUT

FAULT

CROSS-CUT

WATER

LEVERS

BELMAN HOLE VEIN

PADDY END OLD VEIN

GREY CRAG LEVEL

1

2

ROCK FALLS

GREY CRAG LEVEL
North from Paddy End Shaft.

PADDY END SHAFT

MAN HOLE

0    90    180 FT

64

(approximately 210 feet below), to Middle Level about 180 feet above. Much debris has come down from above and has piled up in an alarming amount on floor timbers over the wide shaft, which was really a timbered portion of stope below Grey Crag Level. The copper carbonate coating on the rock and woodwork hereabouts is really quite striking and should be left for others to see. A hair raising view into the yawning chasm under one's feet may be obtained through the man-hole indicated in Figs. 8 and 29. It is quite apparent that an enormous weight of debris lies on the floor timbers. The bottom was found to be strewn with fallen rock and shattered timber in a most unpleasant manner. A tiny portion of a level in a small unworked pillar might be Deep Level, though it seems scarcely deep enough.

An ebullient attempt to scale the shaft, from Grey Crag Level up to Middle Level, utilising an alloy extension ladder, and climbing aids, discovered that at about 140 feet it was dangerously choked with loose rock. A 'window' in one side gave a glimpse into the blackness of a huge stope. Later, when members of the Cumbria Amenity Trust (a mining history society) were completing a successful descent of the upper Paddy End workings, from Levers Water down to Grey Crag Level, the writer and P.Fleming were able to look through this window and recognise the position to which they had climbed months before.

This dramatic descent commences from the bank of Levers Water, at the Back Strings, and unravels its way down through very old workings, over rock falls and false floors, into the Paddy End Vein, down to Middle Level and via Belman Hole Vein down to Grey Crag - a total vertical descent of perhaps 413 feet.(Fig. 30) is a diagrammatical longitudinal section of this trip. It has to be pointed out however, that it is not the intention of this field guide to provide detailed descriptions of explorations and descents into difficult complicated and often very dangerous parts, of the mineworkings.

**WARNING.** A serious fall from the roof of the mine (leaving a crater at the surface) has buried the 'exit' at the foot of the final pitch, now no longer 70 feet! It is still possible to scramble down the debris into Grey Crag Level running off below Levers Water (see Fig.29). The descent of the through-trip can be completed via the upper part of the Paddy End Engine Shaft referred to above. Loose material at the top of this, approx. 140 feet descent, creates a danger,however.

It is recommended that those intending to explore the workings use electron ladder with lifeline, or, S.R.T. leaving ropes in position for return prussik.

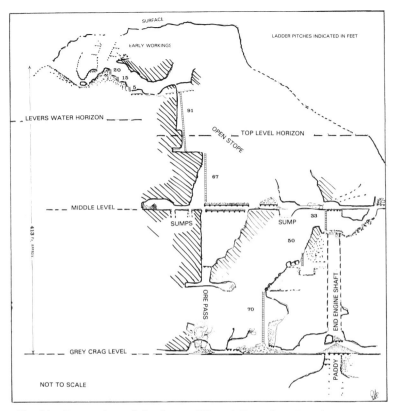

*Fig. 30. Impression of the Levers Water/ Grey Crag Level through descent.*

A 'weighty' question-mark hangs over the lower part of the through-trip: further falls are possible! A solution would be to dig through the blockage...this could be achieved.

Grey Crag level now becomes possessed of a roof of solid rock - almost an anachronism in these strange, gaunt, and yet often beautiful workings. Belman Hole Vein, seemingly barren at this horizon, is followed for some distance to a Y junction. The right-hand branch has been taken as a cross-cut, for some 485 feet, to intersect and explore the Bonsor Vein, which continues (variously known as Bonsor, Fleming's or Thriddle Vein) north-westwards from the great Cross-course at Red Dell or Thriddle. A drive along the vein for a couple of hundred feet, or so, together with a short side passage, showed it to be pretty much worthless-at least hereabouts!

Still using Fig. 29, it will be seen that the left branch at the Y junction soon swings round into a N-S clay-vein or fault which becomes blocked with breakdown material after about 185 feet from the sharp, walled bend. A climb up through loose stuff at the blockage gained entry into a quite imposing stope on the Old Paddy End Vein. Here there is an exceedingly alarming remnant of a masonry 'bunnin', and one also tends to keep a wary eye on a most unstable pinnacle of rock - an inverted 'Sword of Damocles'!

The level continues a long way past the blockage but could well be repeatedly obstructed ..... it remains to be seen.

A little eastwards of the Paddy End Offices indicated on Fig. 26, is the rather picturesque portal of Gaunt's Level. This is safe enough but progress is stopped at 106 yards by a blockage at which point it enters the Kernal Vein.

Many years ago, a short level was put in, just behind the smithy, to try the South Vein. This is however, run-in.

The Paddy End Incline (study Fig. 31) is clearly seen running up below the N.E. face of Grey Crag - the crag itself here indicating the strike of the Paddy End Vein. The further continuation of this important lode is marked by the conspicuous cleft or fissure in the cliff at the head of the valley, adjacent to Levers Water Waterfall. This is Simon's Nick: Simon, as legend would have us believe, sold his soul to the Devil in exchange for riches in copper.

The incline terminates at a small floor on which was fixed, either vertically or horizontally, a large diameter sheaved wheel and drum fitted with a powerful brake operated manually by means of a long lever. The incline worked on the self-acting principle whereby a loaded mine waggon, securely positioned onto a specially designed trolley, was able to haul an empty waggon and its trolley up the incline, as it ran downwards. The trolleys were connected by a long wire rope which passed around the sheaved wheel and these ran on rails. All the operator had to do was to release the locking device preventing the loaded trolley from moving prematurely and apply the brake to maintain an acceptable speed and, of course, to stop the descending trolley at the bottom - this being indicated by the arrival of the empty at the top. The rails were probably single track and if so there would have been a passing place half way down, this being effected by doubling the track. The beauty of an arrangement like this is that there are no fuel bills.

TOP LEVEL →

← MIDDLE LEVEL

←GREY CRAG
LEVEL

E.H.

*Fig. 31    Levers Water Beck at Paddy End showing the incline,
wire rope from Red Dell Foot, and Hospital Level.*

The incline was set-up to bring down ore from the Middle Level. Ore
from the Top Level (the spoil heaps of which can be seen below
Simon's Nick) was originally carted down until connection was made
and ore-passes constructed, between Top and Middle Levels. The ore

was trammed out of Middle Level (entrance now collapsed as is Top Level) along a wooden framework, and tipped into a hopper at the head of the incline. Here the Paddy End Vein is to be observed in outcrop but is cut off and shifted considerably westwards by the Thriddle, Kernal or Great Cross-course.

The incline was dismantled in 1877. A little earlier it would have been possible to look up the valley and see loaded carts bringing ore away from a hopper adjacent to Top Level mouth - these passing over a stone bridge directly below the Levers Water Waterfall; waggons being trammed from Middle Level to the incline hopper; the incline in action; horses drawing waggons from Grey Crag Level and across a bridge by the incline foot; waggons being brought out of Hospital Level and all this ore being taken to the nearby dressing floors. The precise date of closure of the floors is not clear but it was not too many years after the Deep Level came up underneath the Paddy End workings.

There are three other trials (caves) in the Simon Nick cliff. The one at its South-westerly extremity, quite well up, contains a deep flooded sump on a vein, and 25 yards across, southerly from this, are entrances to two short trial tunnels also on this vein.

On the top of the Simon Nick cliff we will find ourselves amongst the workings on the Back Strings where there are a number of ancient ore dressing floors, often adjacent to ruined cabins or 'hutts'. Here the ore was cobbed by hand with the best stuff being taken away by pack-horse direct to Keswick. The poor grades were taken to the stamp-mill at Red Dell Foot (already referred to). It will be seen from Fig. 7 that there are some eight veins in the vicinity, some of which bifurcate.

The visitor is advised to content himself by looking only. The floors of these fissures are in fact the roofs (all supported on ancient timbers) of workings which fall for hundreds of feet below. *It is NOT SAFE to descend them - it is HIGHLY DANGEROUS!*

Paddy End Vein - which can be traced through the Back Strings - courses north-westerly, along the south-westerly margin of Levers Water, to outcrop on the side of Little How Crags not too far to the south west of the Bonsor Vein and the Black Scar Workings.

The Levers Water mine dam has been modified by the water authority, and an arrangement of penstocks and electrically operated valves has been installed in the old egress tunnel. This tunnel was driven during the last century to increase the amount of water available from the tarn - it was equipped with a valve. It emerged in the bed of the tarn about 30 feet below the overflow allowing, as one can see, a very large quantity of water to be held.

The new installation directs a proportion of the outflow into a pipeline feeding - via a pressure-break-tank behind the old smithy - the treatment plant.

Having climbed up the left bank of the beck we can retrace our steps down the Levers Water track. Soon after leaving the overflow, we pass on the left, the cart road over to Glory Hole in Thriddle Scar and then, as we descend, the cart track from Top Level joins from the right, the beck having been crossed remember .... by a stone bridge. Here, too, the main track is crossed by the Top or Kernal Water-race. This gathered from a small wooden dam at the foot of the highest of the waterfalls and it runs along, below Kernal Crag, passing an early working on the Kernal Vein, to deliver in the lagoon at the old Red Dell Mill - thence to the New Engine Shaft wheel. If time permits, follow the race along until the Red Dell works just come into sight, when small grassed-over heaps may be seen on the northernside of the race. These indicate the entrance to a low drift, put through boulder clay, ending at a shaft. This is on the western extension of the Thriddle Vein and is in fact an early air-shaft which ventilated the backs in Flemings's Level. When no longer needed it was fitted with a timber seal.

Immediately below the race, amongst the ruckle of boulders, can be made out the remains of stout masonry pillars. These carried guide wheels for a heavy wire rope, (installed 1877) from the New Engine Shaft winch, to the Middle Level at Paddy End - a considerable distance. In addition, a line of wooden frames, belay pins and snatch-block chains, can be followed in a line to Middle Level. Where it crossed the ravine the rope was carried on steel towers supporting sheave wheels; their stone foundations are still in position. The rope ran into and along Middle Level, down the Paddy End Engine Shaft and raised kibbles up to Deep Level - from deeper workings. Study Fig. 31.

## Route 4
**Brim Fell route**

We will approach the next area to be visited by following the water-race adjacent to Grey Crag Level, along below the crag, (the crag indicates the strike of the Great Cross-course) until its connection with Low Water Beck. The disused compressed-air pipeline, which supplied air from the mines compressor to the Old Man Slate Quarries, runs by here and a little search will reveal the take-off valve which delivered air into a former pipeline taking air to a small venture - John 'Willie' Shaw's Level -high up on the side of Brim Fell at about the 1600 feet contour.

The water-works contractors used this pipe to deliver water down to their site. This is why the pipe is severed and also why modern couplings have been used here and there. The large and very obvious boulder near to the southern bank of Low Water Beck is the Pudding Stone and not very far away, nestling in Pudding Stone Cove, is the grey spoil-heap from Brim Fell Level - a trial on the Brim Fell Vein. Completely safe, the first 48 feet being masonry arched, this fine spacious tunnel was taken in for some 270 feet only to discover that the vein here was merely a quartz string ... with no copper.

Almost directly above here can be seen the discoloured scree of spoil from a very ancient working believed to be John Dixon's Works. Here, a Mr Day made further trial using air drills - driving a cross-cut for about 30 feet and then for 60 feet along the vein; the results were unfavourable. John Dixon's old stope is just above and is about 27 ft in length. Drill holes in the stope might have been for plug and feather, or a small extra trial by Day, using powder.

John 'Willie' Shaw's Level is reached by proceeding along the base of the crag to a further spoil heap best noted perhaps, by lengths of rusty air-pipes. Climb up at this point and the level will hardly be missed. The corrugated-iron shed which housed his tiny smithy is now in ruins. A little above it is a small shelter which served as the explosive cache. The tunnel is spacious and some 336 feet in length, and, like the other two below, it is quite safe. Although driven along the vein, little copper was found, though there was no shortage of iron-pyrites and mispickel. The vein can be seen in outcrop above the tunnel mouth and a few shots have been fired on it. Although Shaw had some help, much of the work was done single-handed using a Schram wet drilling machine and dynamite.

Back now down the steep rough path and follow the crag along to yet another tunnel with a small spoil-heap and the remains of a little cabin. This tunnel is flooded with several feet of slime, *and should not be entered, because a mud filled sump in its floor would prove very dangerous.* In the rock above, the vein is seen in outcrop and carries some copper.

By carrying on, below Raven Tor, up this shallow valley one arrives in due course at Levers Water adjacent to the Back Strings - already described. At this juncture descent may be made, of course, down through Paddy End.

However, by scanning the scree high up on the side of Brim Fell End, (at 2760.9887) a spoil heap almost lost amongst the natural detritus, is from Brim Fell End Level. It marks a hand driven trial by miner John 'Willie'; it proved very poor. Taken in for some 66 feet (along what is likely the Brim Fell Vein) it is quite safe, though perhaps not worth the effort of the climb up!

At an even greater altitude, a remarkable ferruginous (gossany) vein courses over, behind Raven Tor, into Brim Fell Haws where you would be looking down onto the remarkably blue tarn - Low Water. This tarn supplied water to a pelton-wheel driving a generator to provide power for the disued Old Man Slate Quarries.

## Route 5
## Tilberthwaite Region - Wetherlam, Hellen's, Man Arm Borlase Mines et al.

From Coniston, go along the Ambleside Road, turning off up the Tilberthwaite Gill road. Some distance after passing through the fell gate/cattle grid, note up on the left remains of buildings and extensive spoil-heaps. These are mostly of slate quarry spoil or rid, but our by now well practiced eyes should be able to pick out the yellowy brown tips denoting a mineral working - these are in part buried by the slate waste. This is, or was, the Penny Rigg Copper Mill (Study Fig. 32) and ore was brought out to here through the Horse Crag Level (Tilberthwaite Deep Adit) which was driven in for over 3,240 feet to reach the veins of the Tilberthwaite Mine. Its entrance is easily located in the lowest slate quarry - Horse Crag Quarry - and it will be found to be contemporaneously approximately 604 feet in length to where it is blocked by loose clayey material. (Fig. 33). At that point it is almost below the gill. This is a zone of substantially smashed, faulted, and altered, country-rock. Enthusiastic digging might (sic) clear a way through.

Today's explorer may be surprised to enter a sizeable cavern part way along the level. This is an underground slate working or closehead. The shotholes in the tunnel are clearly hand-bored but those in the closehead are seen to be mostly machine drilled. The slate was worked by John W. Shaw after his monumental undertaking on Brim Fell came to an abrupt end after his financier decided that enough money had been wasted. Instead he was franchised to open up here and with the help of a couple of men he remained until he became too old. They probably reserved the workings for the winter months. Air for the drill was supplied by an old ungainly paraffin-engined compressor.

The entrance to the level is wet but the mine is safe to explore.

Water for the Penny Rigg Mill was last brought by an extraordinarily lengthy channel all the way from a small dam across Crook Beck at G.R. 2992.0053, almost opposite Wetherlam Mine. The leat runs down above the southern bank of Tilberthwaite Gill and now does duty as a popular hikers' path.

Quite easily located is another tunnel, adjacent to the mill, named Quarry Adit. (Fig. 34) There is a built-up pond bay formerly feeding a 32 feet in diameter primary-wheel, which was housed in the 35 feet by 5 feet 6 inches by 14 feet deep wheel pit. From this follow the feed-race back to an isolated heap of slate spoil. At the back of this,

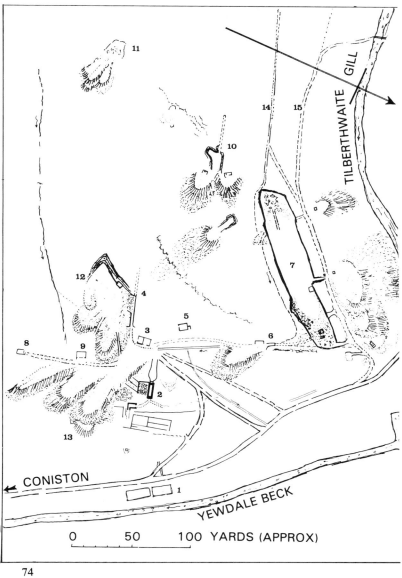

TILBERTHWAITE GILL

11

10

14    15

12    4

7

5

3    6

8    9

2

13

← CONISTON

1

YEWDALE BECK

0    50    100  YARDS (APPROX)

74

Fig. 32    Plan of the region adjacent to Penny Rigg Copper Mill and Quarry.

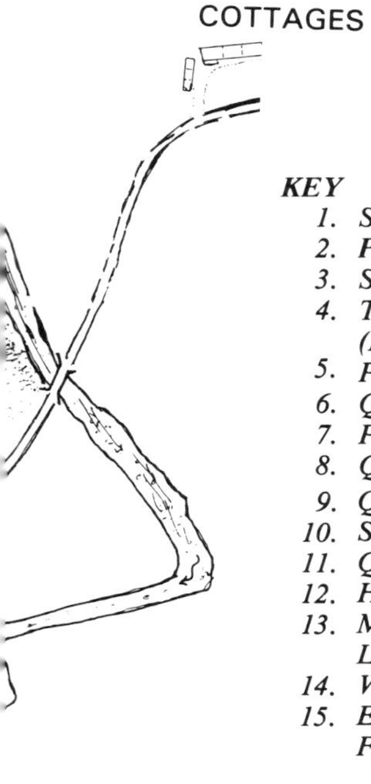

COTTAGES

*KEY*
1. *SETTLING PITS*
2. *PENNY RIGG MILL*
3. *SMITHY AND OFFICE*
4. *TILBERTHWAITE DEEP ADIT LEVEL (HORSE CRAG LEVEL)*
5. *POWDER MAGAZINE*
6. *QUARRY ADIT*
7. *PENNY RIGG QUARRY (SLATE)*
8. *QUARRY MAGAZINE*
9. *QUARRY HUT*
10. *SMALL QUARRY AND LEVEL*
11. *QUARRY AND LEVELS*
12. *HORSE CRAG QUARRY*
13. *MILL SPOIL OVERLAIN BY LATER QUARRY RID*
14. *WATER-RACE FROM CROOK BECK*
15. *EARLIER WATER-RACE FROM FROM THE GILL*

E.H.

in a 37 feet long cutting, is the level mouth. This was driven by hand, from both ends, and running from the lower end of the old Penny Rigg Slate Quarry, it drains that working. The quarry entrance is now blocked, and a partial run-in some way along the tunnel, complicates exploration slightly. This is loose material from the fault, or fissure, along which the tunnel has been partly driven. The fault forms the northern end of the quarry.

Scrambling up from the mouth of the tunnel one soon finds oneself climbing up parallel to the eastern side of the quarry itself, and it is possible, depending on the bracken, to make out the course of the water leat which ran down past the tunnel mouth, to the mill. At the top, or southern end, of the quarry, Wetherlam will be found to dominate the scene ahead rather grandly. Just over to the left is the topmost of the slate workings, above the Horse Crag Quarry, and at the back of it a hand drilled tunnel has been taken in for some 111 feet and this will be found to be completely safe. Below here, in the Penny Rigg Quarry, a tunnel has been taken in to a closehead. This tunnel, however, runs through loose material and is in a *very unsafe condition* and about to collapse - therefore keep out.

Here at the southern end of the quarry one is faced with a choice of routes. The quarry cart-track, which follows the western side of the quarry, forks here. For the purpose of this expedition the reader is required to take the left-hand branch up along the Crook Beck Water-race. However, we can divert to have a look at several interesting features along the other branch, which tends to run straight on. This itself was also a water-race, bringing water from above the first waterfall in the Gill. After passing the 'Clive Eric Samson memorial seat', the path drops steeply down to the first footbridge across the Gill torrent. Now from the bridge, on the same side, go upstream for 40 yards., then up the bank for some 50 feet where the entrance to a tunnel can be found. The water leat was brought along the side of the Gill and through this tunnel, which is driven parallel to the Gill. The upper end is masonry lined but blocked and it is now about 165 feet in length and safe enough. Other details of the leat between here and the collecting point have been eliminated by numerous land-slips.

Years ago, when the Penny Rigg Quarry was much less elongated than it is now, it was worked through the course of this water-race. in compensation for which at some subsequent date, the Crook Beck Race was constructed.

By all means have a look at the dramatic view from the footbridges, but please return to the fork at the top of the quarry, and proceed up

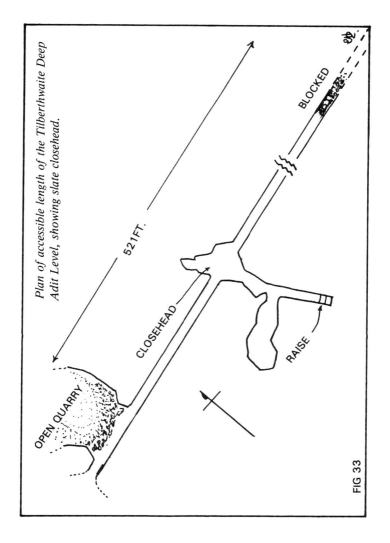

*Plan of accessible length of the Tilberthwaite Deep Adit Level, showing slate closehead.*

OPEN QUARRY

521FT.

CLOSEHEAD

CLOSEHEAD

BLOCKED

RAISE

FIG 33

77

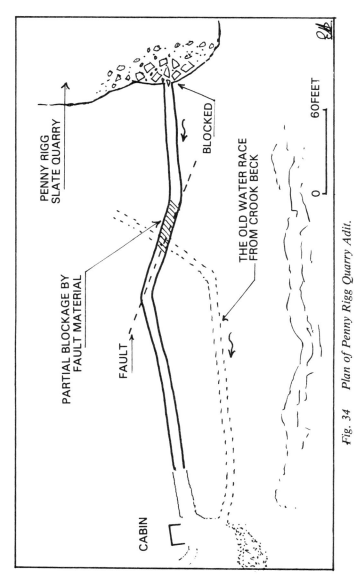

PENNY RIGG SLATE QUARRY

BLOCKED

PARTIAL BLOCKAGE BY FAULT MATERIAL

FAULT

THE OLD WATER RACE FROM CROOK BECK

CABIN

0    60 FEET

*Fig. 34    Plan of Penny Rigg Quarry Adit.*

The water from this race was trained down along the eastern edge of the quarry to join up with the earlier Gill Race channel which had been cut off. However, at some period prior to 1875 when the quarry was probably abandoned, but the mill still in operation, the water was diverted to allow it to cascade over the top of the quarry. Sinking down through the debris it debouched from the mouth of Quarry Adit. A sluice-gate was fitted at the quarry end which, when closed, enabled the quarry to become a reservoir.

The water from the Horse Crag Level was culverted into the primary-wheel feed, and a beck to the south of Horse Crag Quarry was 'captured' and led across by means of a ditch.

After following the Crook Beck Race for some distance it will be seen to pass the entrance cutting to an old mine marked 'Old Level Copper' on the map, (see Fig. 35) which is just above the bend in the gill. This working consists of a tunnel, wet though safe enough, driven in using the ubiquitous jumper and gunpowder. After 180 feet it intersects a poor vein which is apparent upon the surface and upon which, 44 yards above the tunnel mouth, there is also to be found a small open trial and a trench. Beyond for some 32 yards (bearing slightly to the right) a tiny trial has been blasted in a small rock scar, and a search (still bearing right a little) reveals a strong quartz vein streaking along almost to the bend in Crook Beck.

In the shallow soggy defile to the left of 'Old Level Copper' is a 10ft wide by 104ft long peat filled trench which, judging from its spoil, was either a rock cutting in its entirety or had a shallow tunnel driven in at its upper end. Four other smaller trenches are hard by.

From the old copper level continue along the path/water-race, noting after 42 yards, a trial blast in a mineralised outcrop by the side of the path. Below here on the edge of the gill is an ancient open-work on a lead/zinc bearing vein. Underneath this in the cliff is a small level taken in for a few yards to try this same vein. The rock side has been stripped down with explosives to expose the lode better and permit greater observation. A short distance upstream is a much larger stope, about 30 feet high and 27 feet in length, having one or more tunnels off from it. This is also shown on the map as 'Old Level Copper'.

The water-race cum hikers' path continues along to the remains of the dam across Crook Beck, which cascades into the gill near its head.

At the head of Tilberthwaite Gill an adit was put in, many years ago,

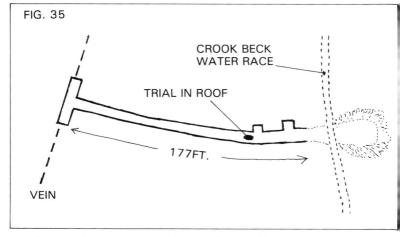

*Fig. 35    Old Level Copper (above Tilberthwaite Gill).*

near the foot of the waterfall. Gill Head Waterfall Level, see Fig. 36, follows a fault plane up along below the bed of the beck. The first few yards are quite old and a trial has been taken off for about 41 feet to the left to try what is considered to be Benson's South Vein or Lode - little ore was found. A little past this branch is a sump down from Benson's Vein Level above and this pours water in wet weather. Eighty feet further a roof collapse has to be climbed over and although the tunnel appears perhaps, worse than it really is, it cannot be considered really safe. The level was extended during the 19th Century to unwater deepening workings upon the lodes at Tilberthwaite Mine further upstream. Cleared again during the 1930's the timber put in has decayed allowing the roof to fall in places. It would prove most interesting if ever the blockages could be cleared and the workings reached. On the left of the entrance to the tunnel a quartz vein may be seen. This is probably Spedding's Lode and there are some 16, narrow diameter holes (plug and feather) drilled into it at this point. There may have been an earlier intention to start a level along it or perhaps the miners stripped it down to get a better look. Spedding's Lode lies directly south of Benson's South Lode and this will be apparent from studying map Fig. 37 which covers this area. It can be seen for example, that along it there is a trial (dig) and a short tunnel beyond which it can be traced further. More about this later.

80

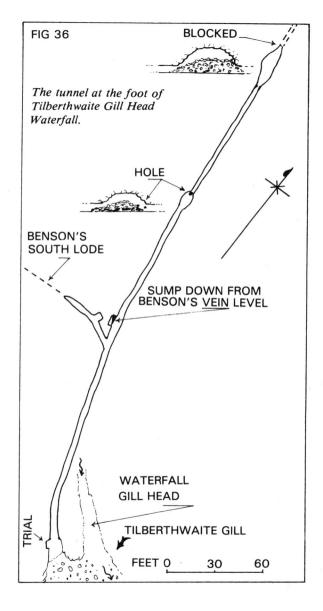

FIG 36

BLOCKED

*The tunnel at the foot of Tilberthwaite Gill Head Waterfall.*

HOLE

BENSON'S SOUTH LODE

SUMP DOWN FROM BENSON'S <u>VEIN</u> LEVEL

WATERFALL GILL HEAD

TRIAL

TILBERTHWAITE GILL

FEET 0    30    60

Upstream from the gill head waterfall, in the western bank by the old ford, a level has been taken in in early times along Benson's Lode. A blocked sump near the entrance drops down into Gill Head Level below. In wet conditions water gathered by this tunnel, from the swollen river, sinks through the choked sump and cascades down into the adit level beneath. Benson's Vein Level is blocked by a fall after only 34 feet. On the surface it may be re-entered through an ancient open-work exhibiting numerous plug and feather grooves. From the far end of this hole the tunnel may be followed along for another 84 feet to a 12 feet high stope with a 19 feet deep sump. How attractive these greeny depths are - but they can drown the unwary!

On the surface again the vein may be traced along small open works to a conspicuous cleft in a small crag - and beyond that. Clearly this is very old, and note near the rock 'pavement' below the cleft, the remains of an old miners' cabin - one of several in the region.

Forty-nine yards upstream from Benson's a 10 feet long trial has been driven into the opposite bank. The intention was to cut a vein running almost parallel to the beck. Above, on the bank, a 22 yards long trench completed the investigation ..... the iron stained vein did not carry enough copper to warrant a bigger attempt.

A further 67 yards upstream on this same side a shallow adit was put in, either to drain early shallow workings a little north of here, or to prospect them, or both. Just around the next bend in the beck is the Tilberthwaite Mine itself. Here the 'office', smithy, wheel-housing, copper sheds and other structures - as well as the extensive open workings on the North Lode - can be identified. The square pit adjacent to the beck is a blocked shaft on the Shaft Lode. At the extreme eastern end of the North Lode, an irregular ladder-shaft connecting with the Horse Crag or Tilberthwaite Deep Adit Level some 540 feet below, 'nipped-in' at the top during early 1971. Utmost care needs to be taken in the resulting depression. The old open stopes and collapses on the North Lode can be traced 206 feet or so to the currently deepest hole which is close to the pretty cascade on the beck. The vein is seen to cross the beck and may be followed up along a small escarpment, with which it appears to correspond, with several small diggings along its length. There is a small, not very obvious, underground working along here too. North Lode Trial Mine (writer) consists of a 21 feet long cross-cut then a drift along the vein for about 42 feet. It showed the vein to be of no consequence at that location and the working, of some age, is quite safe. Generally the North Lode strikes towards the God's Blessing Vein where the latter sweeps over the southern flanks (Lower Hows) of Wetherlam.

There was at least one water-wheel at the Tilberthwaite Mine and the simple race which delivered to the small pond or bay was but a short affair taking its water from the cascade. From the pond (which could be emptied into the beck) it was fed to the wheel by a wooden flume. The wheel likely powered a roll-crusher and a small set of stamps; possibly other equipment such as a round buddle. It might also have been called upon to wind kibbles up the shaft on Shaft Lode. In early times a horse-gin might have been used for this duty though there is little evidence to confirm this, or, if there had been one, when it became disused. Whatever plant was here, no matter what condition it was in, it would have been rendered obsolete when Tilberthwaite Deep Adit Level was driven up below and the mill at Penny Rigg put into commission. Even so the site, like the Penny Rigg Mill, apart from damage during scrap metal recovery and more recently by the usual 'touroid' vandals, remains pretty much as it was in the 1800's.

Postlethwaite writes in his 'Mines and Mining in the Lake District', that about £10,000 was spent developing the mine, including the Horse Crag Level, '.... but the returns did not exceed half that sum.'

About half-way down the cascade a wooden barrier formerly diverted water into a well-contructed leat on the opposite bank, which had a fair storage capacity. The leat can be followed to a large boulder which has been blasted with gunpowder where there would have been two sluice gates. One gate drew off unwanted water along a small channel to a point where it was allowed to run down into the beck - it will be seen that it has scoured away a large segment. The other gate delivered water into another leat running roughly parallel to the beck, to a position only 18 feet from the old surface working on Benson's Lode. Here, the writer believes, was located an early 17th Century stamping mill belonging to the Society of Mines Royal. The site may also have been used by subsequent operators - this is indicated by the blasted boulder. Although traces of any obvious structure have vanished, diligent search revealed building stones apparently split by plug and feather; there also appears to be a tail-race. A track (pony?) runs from this place back to the square shaft on the Shaft Lode. The beck would have been crossed by a wooden bridge and investigation revealed holes drilled in either bank to take holding down pins.

Some 18 yards from the cascade - uphill from the stamp mill leat - is an ancient rock cutting some 30 feet in length by 18 inches wide. Fifteen yards from this is a 42 feet long prospecting trench. Both are upon narrow veins and the one nearest the cascade can be seen

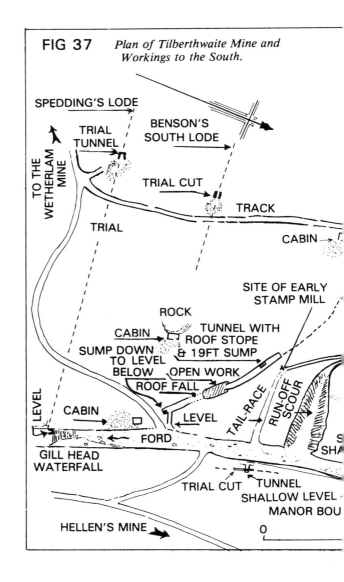

**FIG 37** *Plan of Tilberthwaite Mine and Workings to the South.*

SPEDDING'S LODE

TRIAL TUNNEL

BENSON'S SOUTH LODE

TO THE WETHERLAM MINE

TRIAL CUT

TRACK

TRIAL

CABIN

SITE OF EARLY STAMP MILL

ROCK

CABIN

TUNNEL WITH ROOF STOPE & 19FT SUMP

SUMP DOWN TO LEVEL BELOW

OPEN WORK

ROOF FALL

LEVEL

CABIN

LEVEL

TAIL-RACE

RUN-OFF SCOUR

FORD

S SHA

GILL HEAD WATERFALL

TRIAL CUT

TUNNEL SHALLOW LEVEL MANOR BOU

HELLEN'S MINE

0

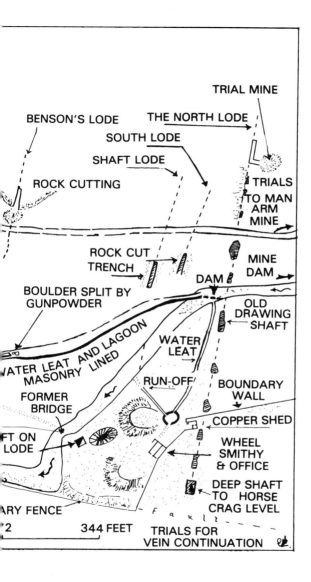

BENSON'S LODE

THE NORTH LODE

TRIAL MINE

SOUTH LODE

SHAFT LODE

ROCK CUTTING

TRIALS

TO MAN ARM MINE

ROCK CUT TRENCH

MINE DAM

DAM

BOULDER SPLIT BY GUNPOWDER

OLD DRAWING SHAFT

WATER LEAT AND LAGOON MASONRY LINED

WATER LEAT

RUN-OFF

BOUNDARY WALL

FORMER BRIDGE

COPPER SHED

FT ON LODE

WHEEL SMITHY & OFFICE

DEEP SHAFT TO HORSE CRAG LEVEL

ARY FENCE

fault

2          344 FEET

TRIALS FOR VEIN CONTINUATION

85

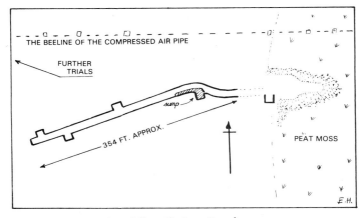

*Fig 38    Man Arm Mine. Bottom Level.*

crossing the beck lower down; this is probably Shaft Lode. The other is not so clear in this direction and seems not to have a name. Both can be traced with ease though, through and beyond the track passing by above here. Both are ancient.

A short distance up-stream from the cascade is the mine dam. This held back a considerable, though shallow, lake occupying Dry Cove Bottom - a misnomer if ever there was! Originally the dam was to have been much higher: evidence of this is a distinct channel running from its eastern end directly down towards the dressing floor.

From the dam walk across to Dry Cove Fold (sheep-fold) at G.R. 2966.0103 which is just below the confluence of Swallow Scar and Henfoot becks. From here along the base of Wetherlam to Man Arm Mine (Fig. 38), and its grey spoil heaps, at 2943.0117. This is one of the old mines which was investigated by the Greenburn and Tilberthwaite Mining Company while operated hereabouts in the 1930's. It was named, so it is said, because of the 'kink' in the main or Bottom Level. This was taken in for some 350 feet with about 30 feet of side passages. The floor is under-stoped in places, and is water covered, thus alertness is required to avoid a ducking - or worse. The company opened up the vein above here by two trials, one of which is a short tunnel 27 feet in length. There are quite good shows of ore but not, it would seem, in quantities worth exploiting. A paraffin-engined air-compressor was brought up to one of their nearby mines and machine drills were used to do some of the work at

86

Man Arm. The small cairns of rock down from the upper trials were supports for the air-line. Its further course can be traced across the peat-moss by means of wooden stakes set into the swampy ground. This area is shown in map Fig. 39.

*Stakes carried the air pipe across the peat bog to Man Arm Mine.*

From Man Arm Mine, a compass bearing of 57 degrees points at the yellow/brown waste from Hellen's Mine, which we shall visit later, along with Borlase Mine where the compressor was stationed.

Northerly from Man Arm, at an altitude of 1,625ft., is a working (at 2935.0154) which might logically, in view of its location, be named Birk Fell Hause Mine. Its spoil falls for a long way down the steep fell and it is believed to be of some antiquity. Barytes was located here by the writer - a most uncommon mineral in these fells. The lowest level (by the old cabin) is still open, though wet, but only runs in for a few feet. Above is another level, and a length of stope but both are collapsed. Beyond, the vein may be seen quite strongly with several open-cuts along it. The largest of these, according to W.T.Shaw, yielded several tons of erubescite some 80 years ago. This suggests the Coniston Mining Syndicate, active herabouts, around the turn of the century. By following the vein up further still one arrives at a sort of 'summit' where it appears to correspond with the Long Crag Vein of the Greenburn assemblage. The valley below is indeed Greenburn but this and its mineral workings are the subject of the next section.

Standing at the Birk Fell Hause Mine once again, and sighting eastwards, one may be able to spot the spoil heaps of Top Level at Borlase Mine; indeed they appear to be on the same contour. Between the two mines, still on the Birk Fell Hause Vein (writer), and positioned betwixt two mountain butresses is a small trial. See if you can find it whilst walking across to Borlase workings.

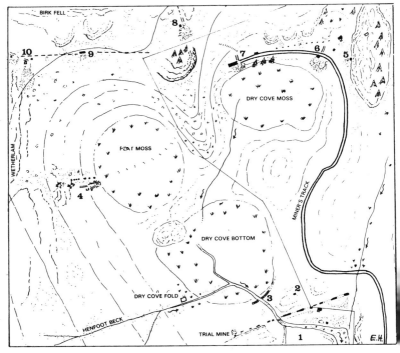

Fig 39   Map showing The Cove North-West of Tilberthwaite
Mine and the Workings above it. Study this in
conjunction with Fig. 49.

1. TILBERTHWAITE MINE
2. TRIAL
3. MINE DAM
4. MAN ARM MINE
5. HAYSTACK LEVEL

6.HELLEN'S MINE
7.BORLASE MINE —
  BOTTOM LEVEL
8.BORLASE MINE —
  TOP LEVEL
9.TRIAL
10.BIRK FELL HAUSE MINE

Top Level of Borlase Mine (see Fig. 40) has recently been re-opened and entry can be effected with a little effort. A small working, there is little danger inside, as the woodwork is still in reasonable condition. The squeeze in at the entrance however, may be a little off-putting to the more faint hearted. It was taken in and along the Borlase Vein which is a 'caunter lode' or one which does not emulate the general direction of other veins in the region. It has been stoped away above and also below the level. The vein can be traced with ease

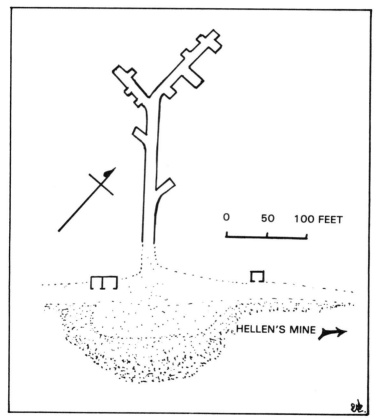

*Fig 41      Borlase Mine - Bottom Level (plan).*

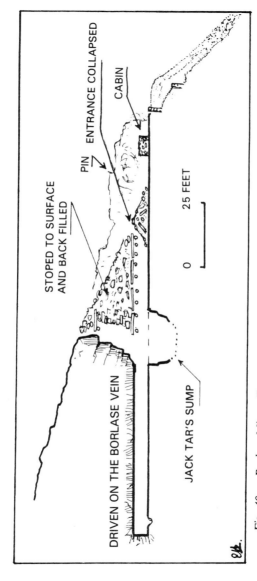

*Fig. 40    Borlase Mine - Top Level (Section).*

ENTRANCE COLLAPSED

CABIN

PIN

STOPED TO SURFACE
AND BACK FILLED

DRIVEN ON THE BORLASE VEIN

JACK TAR'S SUMP

0          25 FEET

striking north-south over the moor into Greenburn and there are several surface workings upon it. After a short distance it appears to cut off or shift an east-west bearing vein of the Greenburn group - possibly Pave York Vein. Shown on Fig.49.

Bottom Level (Fig. 41) at Borlase Mine is lower down and a set of steps, now in bad condition, used to join the two. It was driven in through very hard rhyolite in an intensive search for the vein at this lower horizon but with no success. The working is quite safe and consists of a driveage of approximately 384 feet including numerous side branches (see Fig. 41) indicating the frantic probing to find, one suspects, anything - so long as it was worth working. A large cabin adjacent to the entrance housed the smithy and the air-compressor.

From Borlase Mine a well preserved cart-track climbs gently up to Hellen's Mine with its discoloured spoil heaps and a tiny cabin or two (see Fig. 42). Here a drive was made for 189 feet along what proved to be a very ferruginous vein. A shaft in the roof comes down from an upper, partly surface, working. The main level was hand drilled but with the coming of the compressor an extra side branch was driven along a nearly parallel vein or string for about 69 feet and rock-drills were used for this.

Hellen's Vein may be traced eastwards, past the surface working falling down to the level below and, after passing several trenches, up onto a rock outcrop or knoll where one or two trials have been made. It may be followed down into a curious shallow defile, where trenches and pits are to be seen along the same lode, and eventually to an open stope in a small crag which, with its small cabin and the general aspect of the place, is somewhat engrossing. This working is believed to be Haggrieg's or Hawkrigg's or Walker's Works and is shown on the map as Hawk Rigg. (Study plan Fig. 43). The stope is some 44 feet in length, 2-3 feet across and about 27 feet in depth. A sump in its forebay is some 25 feet in depth but only partly flooded, save during wet conditions when it fills up and decants over. The reason for this is that the water leaks down along fissures into Booth's Level below which was driven in from lower down the hill to investigate the lode at a greater depth. The 291 feet drive, with short side passages, (see Figs. 43 and 44) was a complete disappointment. Dr P.L.Booth of Barrow-in-Furness had the level driven in 1911 and the place is quite safe to explore.

A feature of the old stope which, incidentally, dates back to the early 1600's, is the rainwater channel cut into the rock just above the fissure in order to run away water, so that it would not patter onto the heads of the miners below. Take care not to slip here.

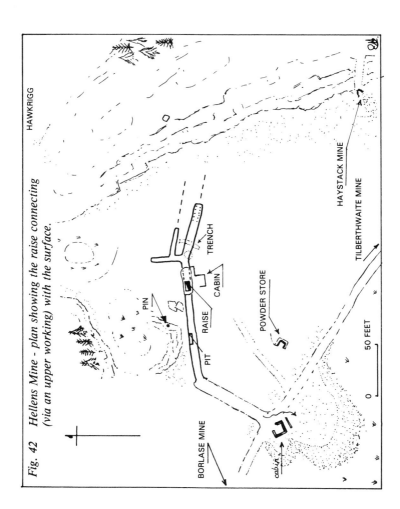

Fig. 42    Hellens Mine - plan showing the raise connecting
(via an upper working) with the surface.

HAWKRIGG

TRENCH

CABIN

PIN

RAISE

PIT

POWDER STORE

BORLASE MINE

cabin

HAYSTACK MINE

TILBERTHWAITE MINE

0        50 FEET

It is fascinating to speculate upon the probability of whether any of these old workings - Benson's Lode, Hawkriggs or the surface workings on the North Lode at the Tilberthwaite Mine - might have been one or more of the 'Three Kings' of the Elizabethan Tyrolean miners.

Some 53 yards north-westerly of the old stope is a blocked trial tunnel or a trench upon another, almost parallel vein. By following this westwards up the defile one arrives at an outcrop working 15 yards from the old boundary fence (see Fig. 43). This vein runs at about 288 degrees and appears to be cut off near, probably by, the Borlase Vein north of the Top Level. This gives rise to the interesting speculation that the vein might be the 'tail-end' of the 280 degrees Pave York Vein of the Greenburn group. This courses along Birk Fell summit and itself appears to be cut off by the Borlase Vein quite near to the Top Level at Borlase Mine.

Having taken all this in and perhaps weary after frantically attempting to locate and trace these lodes for himself the reader might now be prepared to return to the main cart-track at Hellen's Mine. Down it after 45 yards a small crag will be on the left. Haystack Level is another of these ancient trials and is driven in to the base of the cliff for about 24 feet and only 2 feet in width. It is quite safe to enter. The vein it is taken in along is scarcely noticeable.

From the Haystack, carry on down the old mine cart-track and cross the beck by the ford by the mouth of the level driven into Benson's Vein. Walk on along the track until one is practically at the foot of Wetherlam (see map Fig. 45). The track here (2981.0068) forks off to the right and that branch runs along below the conspicuous cleft on Benson's Vein to cross over the two veins (one of these is Shaft Lode) due south of North Lode and then off in the general direction of Dry Cove Sheep-fold. Adjacent to the fork can be seen a small working consisting simply of a 24 feet cutting in the rock and a 12 feet tunnel apparently hand drilled and dynamited. This is upon Spedding's Lode which can be traced from the waterfall at the gill head to here, and past the nearby trial for some distance. It lies about 144 yards south of Benson's Lode but between the two can be seen yet another vein or string with a small rock-cut upon it. This must be Benson's South Lode which has been explored a little from the adit level at the foot of the gill head waterfall.

Continuing along the track, around the bend, and along the base of the mountain for some 133 yards, one will find oneself at yet another lode having about six small trials upon it above the track, the lowest

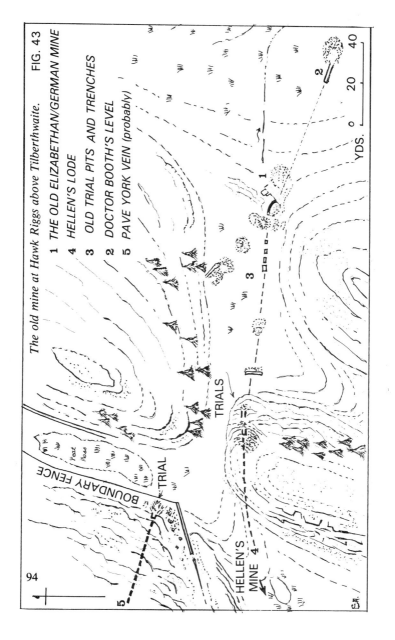

94

The old mine at Hawk Riggs above Tilberthwaite.    FIG. 43

1 THE OLD ELIZABETHAN/GERMAN MINE
4 HELLEN'S LODE
3 OLD TRIAL PITS AND TRENCHES
2 DOCTOR BOOTH'S LEVEL
5 PAVE YORK VEIN (probably)

TRIALS

TRIAL

BOUNDARY FENCE

Peat hags

HELLEN'S MINE    4

5

0    20    40
YDS.

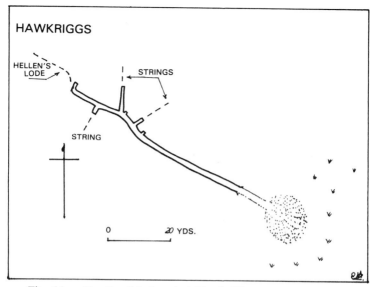

Fig. 44    Dr. Booth's Level at Hawk Riggs.

of which consists of a short cutting and tunnel. Investigation will show that the vein itself has been shifted by faulting in a couple of places but its general strike may be followed by noting the small excavations upon it. Some 20 yards below the track the vein has been explored by a trench and a large rock-cutting. Despite showings of copper, Steel Edge Vein (writer) did not warrant, it seems, the driving of a level for more careful investigation.

A further 120 yards brings us to the Wetherlam Mine itself (see Fig. 46). An object of considerable interest here is the iron horse-gin used in the beginning to wind the kibble up from the floor workings in the level. Collapsed during a heavy downpour in 1973 entry was effected once again during 1979. It can be seen from the section that stoping has been carried out in the roof, and the floor of the level, which has been taken in along the vein. However, as the level is 18 inches or so deep in water the greatest vigilance is called for to avoid falling through the submerged woodwork. The Wetherlam Vein is easily followed from where it is best exposed - just by the side of the cascade above here - to well up the steep and slippery side of the fell.

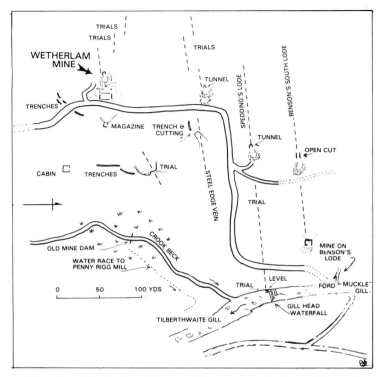

*Fig. 45    Wetherlam Mine and the area to the South-West of Fig. 37*

Some five trials have been made upon it and one of these, at the end of a shallow cut, consists of a small entrance directly into a flooded stope seemingly cut by primitive tools. A little above this is a more recent try involving explosives. The vein is seen (like Steel Edge Vein) to be displaced about three times along its course. The topmost working is probably the ancient Hen Crag or Swallow Scar Working and is just above a small plateau at about the 1,800 feet contour which has the remains of a small miners' 'hutt' upon it. The tunnel is at the back of a deep gulley in the scar. It is taken in for about 22 feet; is about 4 feet in height by 3 feet in width. Entry was made by the writer in 1971 and numerous half-inch grooves suggest that plug and feathers were extensively used in this small unproductive attempt.

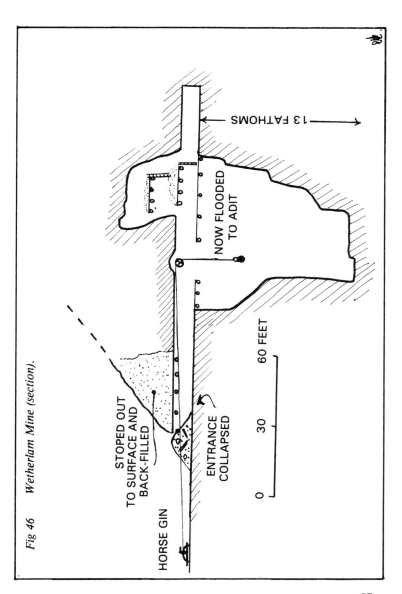

Fig 46    Wetherlam Mine (section).

13 FATHOMS

NOW FLOODED
TO ADIT

STOPED OUT
TO SURFACE AND
BACK-FILLED

ENTRANCE
COLLAPSED

HORSE GIN

0        30        60 FEET

97

In searching for the easterly extension of the Wetherlam Vein (that is below the track) numerous trenches have been dug and some are adjacent to the track itself a little south of the mine spoil. A small cabin against a rock outcrop some 22 yards east of the track (below the mine), was the explosive magazine. Sixty yards downhill from this are still more trenches with a small portion of the vein exposed by blasting. The cabin (having a corrugated iron roof at the time of writing) some 85 yards south of here, probably housed a water pump delivering to the small reservoir feeding the dressing plant up at the mine. Indications show that some item of machinery was formerly bolted to the floor.

Compressed-air was brought all the way from the Coniston Mines compressor to the Wetherlam Mine by a 2 inch diameter pipe installed in 1902. An air-powered hoist was put in the level for winding up the kibble, replacing the horse-gin, whilst a small air pump in the bottom kept the sole dry.

By following the track southwards into Hole Rake an ancient flooded open stope can be seen in the opposite bank of Crook Beck gill. This is marked on the map as 'Copper Level' at 2967.9966 though it is upon a zinc bearing vein, care is needed - if one falls into the flooded hole, one will probably fail to extricate oneself.

East of the track here are the old Moor Slate Quarries - probably worth a look if time permits. By continuing along the track one duly tops the rise and looks rather grandly down into Copper Mines Valley where we started our first tour.

The return trip to the head of Tilberthwaite Gill (there may at some time be installed a footbridge here) can be varied by attempting to trace the course of the air-line from where it came over Hole Rake summit, along the boulder strewn fell-side, to the Wetherlam Mine. Its line is evidenced by tiny rock pillars or cairns, and iron hooks, brackets etc. set into rock masses.

From the top of the gill descend by the cart-track down the northern side of the spectacular ravine. Near the bottom the track passes a small working on a zinc lode where, in the forebay of the short upper level (the bottom level is blocked) a hole drops down into the level below. G.R. 3038.0103.

It was up this same track (now very rough and rain scoured) that haulier Coward from Coniston, and his six strong horses, pulled the heavy compressor for the Borlase Mine. The road carries on down, through the fell-gate, over a tiny ford, around the rear of Low Tilberthwaite cottages, and down in front of them to the surfaced road.

## Route 6
## Greenburn Mine, Pave York Levels, Long Crag Levels etc.

From Little Langdale (parking difficult) cross the River Brathay by footbridge at GR 3158.0287. Follow the track along the southern bank of the river (on foot, there is nowhere to park along here) and continue through Low Hall Garth and High Hall Garth with its fell-gate. The spoil heaps along here are from old slate quarries and these well repay a visit in passing. After High Hall Garth proceed, bearing left at the 'Y' junction, to the fell-gate cum stile at the lower end of Greenburn Valley.

A short distance past this gate note in the opposite bank the mouth of Greenburn Beck Level (Fig. 47) which is reasonably safe to enter. The tunnel forks left after 60 feet running on for some 156 feet. The main drive continues for 174 feet, with stoping in the roof for 18-20 feet, with debris from the latter to be climbed over. The level is seen to be taken along a narrow vein or fault which might well be the Low Gill Vein of the Greenburn group. Cobalt bloom has been noticed in the vein. On the same bank, a little upstream, there is a shallow water-filled trial on the same vein.

The mine site and dressing floors lie a further distance upstream. They are quite well preserved and thus fairly interpretable. (Study Fig. 48). There are 5 veins on the 'sett' the most northerly being the Low Gill Lode, though this does not appear to have been very productive. Sump Lode lies about 200 feet to the south of this and was the most important vein of all; workings were taken down to below 120 fathoms from the eye of Engine Shaft which was itself put down on the vein - all the way in ore. Most likely its line of descent was simply a timbered space down through the worked out stopes with partitioning into two compartments - one for winding the kibble, the other for the pumping gear and a ladder-way. The shaft top can be located amongst the ruins (shown on map Fig. 48) and has an iron pump-rod protruding through the rocks blocking it. The head of the cast-iron rising-main with iron run-off box is also to be seen - beware however, if probing about - the blockage might clear itself without warning. Sump Lode is easily traced on the surface here as it is pin-pointed by the shaft itself, and then by a shallow open cutting adjacent, which also has a 12 feet length of tunnel. The vein can be followed beyond through a rock exposure and just past this, in a wet patch of ground, a hole opens into a deep, flooded, stoped away, portion of the vein. The water level in here will be the same as that in Engine Shaft. Be careful not to fall in as there would be no hope of survival! In fact, the hole locates the position of an

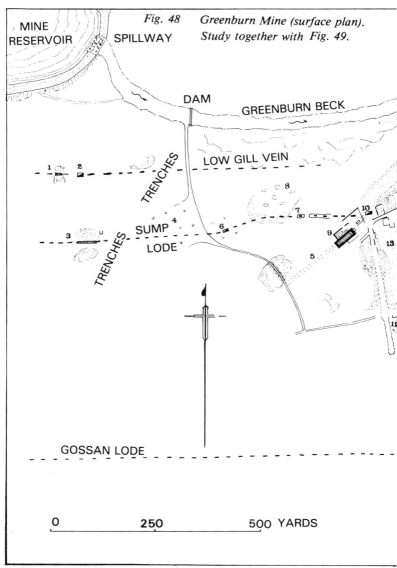

Fig. 48    Greenburn Mine (surface plan).
Study together with Fig. 49.

MINE RESERVOIR    SPILLWAY

DAM

GREENBURN BECK

LOW GILL VEIN

TRENCHES

1    2

8

7    10

SUMP    4

6

3    TRENCHES    9

LODE    5    13

GOSSAN LODE

0    250    500 YARDS

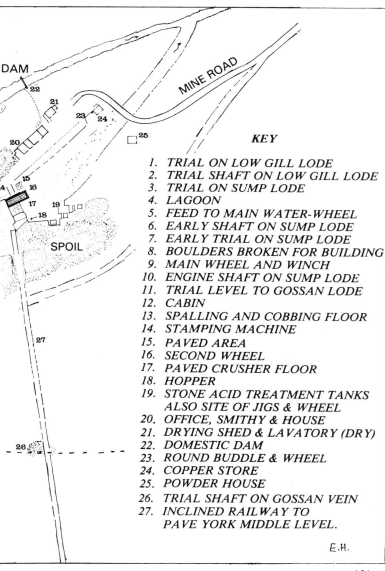

DAM

MINE ROAD

**KEY**

1. TRIAL ON LOW GILL LODE
2. TRIAL SHAFT ON LOW GILL LODE
3. TRIAL ON SUMP LODE
4. LAGOON
5. FEED TO MAIN WATER-WHEEL
6. EARLY SHAFT ON SUMP LODE
7. EARLY TRIAL ON SUMP LODE
8. BOULDERS BROKEN FOR BUILDING
9. MAIN WHEEL AND WINCH
10. ENGINE SHAFT ON SUMP LODE
11. TRIAL LEVEL TO GOSSAN LODE
12. CABIN
13. SPALLING AND COBBING FLOOR
14. STAMPING MACHINE
15. PAVED AREA
16. SECOND WHEEL
17. PAVED CRUSHER FLOOR
18. HOPPER
19. STONE ACID TREATMENT TANKS
    ALSO SITE OF JIGS & WHEEL
20. OFFICE, SMITHY & HOUSE
21. DRYING SHED & LAVATORY (DRY)
22. DOMESTIC DAM
23. ROUND BUDDLE & WHEEL
24. COPPER STORE
25. POWDER HOUSE
26. TRIAL SHAFT ON GOSSAN VEIN
27. INCLINED RAILWAY TO
    PAVE YORK MIDDLE LEVEL.

SPOIL

E.H.

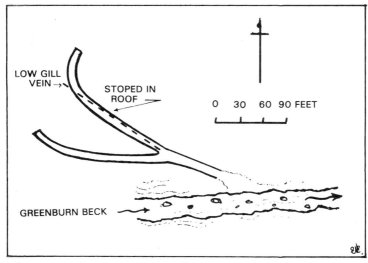

*Fig. 47      Greenburn Beck Level.*

early shaft taken down vertically to the 28 Fathom Level, and deeper still by means of winzes. (Map Fig. 48 should be studied with map Fig. 49).

Above the nearby rock exposure there will be seen a number of shallow holes. These were at first thought by the writer to be searches for the vein but after discovering evidence in the form of a rock drilled but not blasted, and a slice with a shothole groove down one side, the conclusion is that large boulders lying about were broken to provide building material: a great deal of rock was used in the various structures.

A plan of the area, Fig. 49, demonstrates the vein pattern though it must be confessed that this has been simplified - faulting has resulted in discontinuation and shifting. (This map should be considered in conjunction with map Fig. 48).

Water for the mill was conveyed by leat from a catchment area or lagoon which was in turn fed by a short channel from the beck where a barrier diverted the water. A large and well constructed storage reservoir was built some 350 yards west of the works. When required, water was simply run off into the beck. Regretably the dam was breached recently during a severe storm and the water rushed out and down the valley to at least one farmer's consternation. It is to be hoped that some authority, possibly the Lake District Special Planning Board, might at some time in the not too distant future be inclined to restore this valuable and attractive relic - monument as it is to mans' endeavour.

Between the works and this reservoir a trial shaft has been put down on what is believed to be Low Gill Lode. Some ore was found but not enough presumably, to warrant anything more than this shaft a few fathoms deep. Across from this, southerly, about 43 yards away, a trial has been made on the Sump Lode (?). Again not much was found in the way of rich ore. Trenches are to be found on these veins between the works and the mine dam.

A short distance south-easterly of the Sump Lode trial, numerous large rocks will be seen to have been 'shot'. These were blasted to obtain good heavy building stone for the works, the material being brought down by horse drawn cart or sledge.

The pump-rods in the Engine Shaft were fixed to a balance-bob, the decayed remains of which are still to be seen above the shaft. This was rocked by a long reciprocating shaft, either of wood or iron, which was pivoted about mid-way between the shaft and a crank on the primary water-wheel axle or else on the winding winch.

The wheel was housed in a pit 36 feet in length by 4 feet 9 inches wide and 14 feet in depth and was supplied by an elevated wooden launder collecting from the end of the supply leat. A sluice was fixed at this end to enable the water to run away, if so desired, though it was deliberately channelled to supply the final stages of ore washing.

The tail-race from the big wheel (which might have been in the region of 29 feet in diameter) fed another wheel set in a pit 25 feet 6 inches in length by 4 feet 10 inches in width. This powered a battery of stamps on one side and a large jaw crusher on the other. The crusher was hand fed from the terrace above where screening, washing, sorting and spalling, were carried out under cover. After stamping, the low grade stuff was delivered to water-powered jigs, a little downstream. As usual, the best hand-picked material would be ready for market after reducing in size. Jigged ore was taken further down, to water-powered buddles, where it was further concentrated. Adjacent to these operations were the copper storage sheds.

Slime pits were located below the jigs and buddles. Yet there appears to be little sand or slime piled anywhere. It is quite likely that from time-to-time quantities escaped into Greenburn Beck - quite unintentionally, of course.

Fig. 49   Map showing the approximate strike of the Greenburn
          Lodes and the Mines opened up on these. Study in
          conjunction with Fig. 48.

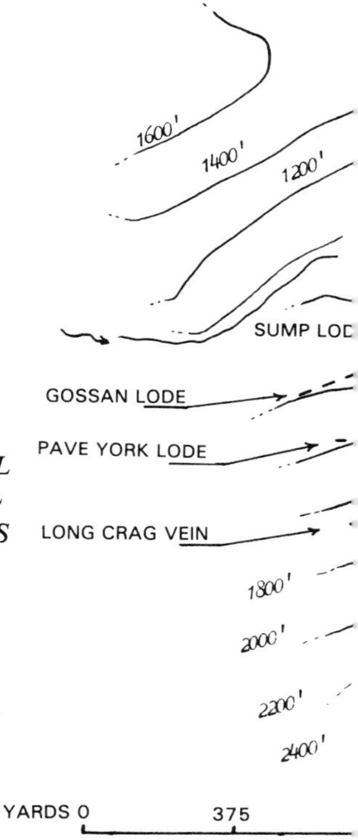

KEY

1. MINE RESERVOIR
2. GREENBURN MINE & MILL
3. GREENBURN BECK LEVEL
4. GREENBURN BECK
5. MINE ROAD
6. GOSSAN VEIN - TRIAL LEVEL
7. GOSSAN VEIN - TRIAL SHAFT
8. INCLINED RAILWAY TO
   PAVE YORK MIDDLE LEVEL
9. PAVE YORK VEIN BOTTOM LEVEL
10. PAVE YORK VEIN MIDDLE LEVEL
11. PAVE YORK VEIN TOP WORKINGS
12. LONG CRAG LEVEL
13. UPPER WORKINGS ON
    LONG CRAG VEIN
14. BIRK FELL HAUSE MINE
15. MAN ARM MINE
16. BORLASE MINE - BOTTOM LEVEL
17. HELLEN'S MINE
18. HAYSTACK LEVEL
19. BORLASE MINE - TOP LEVEL

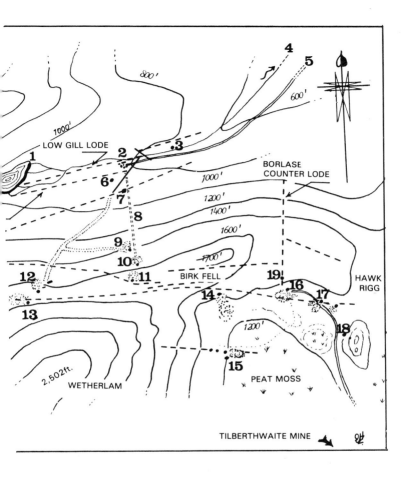

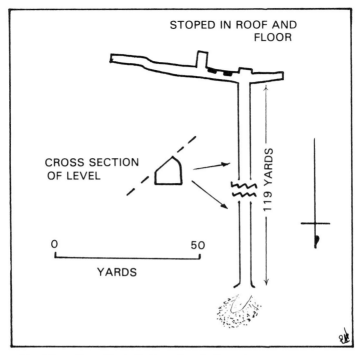

*Fig. 50    Pave York Bottom Level. Greenburn.*

The square stone tanks, originally lead-lined, were used in the treatment of certain ore with sulphuric acid, and the precipitation of the copper with scrap iron.

Enough remains of the house, office and smithy to form an impression of what this site must have looked like at the time of working. A miniature water leat brought water from the beck, diverted by a wooden barrier, and this was probably for domestic use, for the men to wash, and for the blacksmith. Of two further sheds, close to the end of the terrace, one was obviously a dry closet. The other was a drying and changing cabin. A fire, fed from outside, had its hot gases ducted below an iron plate in the floor of the hut. Upon this the miners would have placed their clogs and boots to dry, whilst above, they hung their damp clothing.

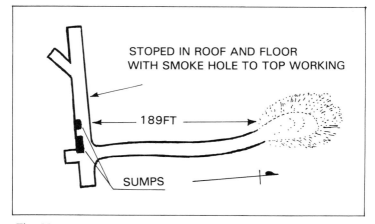

*Fig. 51    Pave York Vein. Middle Level.*

Just above the spalling and sorting floor, a 'causeway' can be seen running to a cutting with a partially blocked level at its far end. This was put in during 1865/6 to prove the Gossan Vein which lies about 100 yards southerly of Sump Lode - indeed we could call this Gossan Vein Cross-cut. About 60 yards in length, and quite safe, it still has wooden rails on its floor; little is to be seen of the vein however, other than one or two narrow quartz strings. The walls and roof are slime covered though and the 4 feet 6 inches or so of cold water standing inside is not conducive to prolonged examination. One would have assumed however, that if the vein had appeared at all promising, the miners would at least have driven along it for some distance. Before the tunnel was driven, a shaft had been sunk (early 1865) on the vein on the surface, uphill from the level mouth. This - Gossan Vein Trial Shaft (writer) had only been taken down for 30 feet before wet conditions caused the project to be abandoned.

The next vein lies about 408 yards south of Gossan and is named Pave York Lode. There are three major workings on this lode, well up the fellside above the mill site. The lowest, Pave York Bottom Level (writer), is shown on the plan Fig. 50, to enter the vein after approximately 357 feet. Workings in here have flooded sumps in the floor and great care is required. About half-way along the adit, the cross-section is unique, for a sloping fault is allowed to form one side of the roof.

Higher still is Pave York Middle Level (writer) and is of interest in

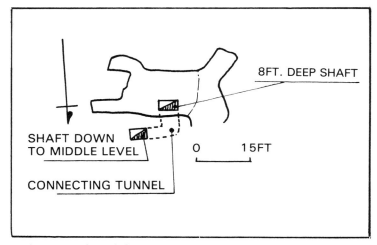

*Fig. 52    Plan of the Top Working on Pave York Vein, Greenburn.*

that wooden rails are still in position. The cross-cut intersects (see Fig. 51) after about 186 feet and the workings on the vein also have flooded sumps in the floor, and again care is needed.

Above this is Pave York Top Level (writer) and this is seen to more resemble a 'cave' with two small tries in it. (Fig. 52). A shallow pit near to the entrance gives into a low tunnel ending in a shaft, a smoke hole, falling into the top of the stope on Pave York Middle Level below. Obviously great care is required.

Formerly a cart road zig-zagged up to the middle level, passing by the mouth of the bottom level. This became defunct above the bottom level in consequence of an inclined railway brought up from the mill. This had wooden rails, re-inforced by iron strips, and was laid where possible upon the ground but also upon built-up masonry lengths. At the bottom it resembles a 'causeway' and it lies 66 feet easterly of the 'causeway' to Gossan Cross-Cut. It was almost certainly a self-acting incline similar to that at Paddy End. Gossan Trial Shaft is passed after climbing 123 yards up the incline.

Above the top trial, to the left, is a small trial on the Pave York Vein which courses visibly over the top of Birk Fell, to where it appears to be cut off by the Borlase Caunter Lode. Shown on Fig. 49.

108

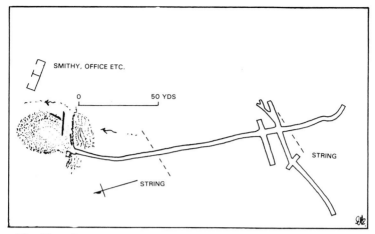

*Fig. 53    Long Crag Level, Greenburn.*

Long Crag Vein is the most southerly of the five, lying about 240 yards south of Pave York Vein. It appears to correspond, the reader may recollect, with the vein upon Birk Fell Hause, from out of a cutting on which several tons of erubescite were obtained. It may be easily followed, as a strong quartz vein, westwards along the rugged mountainside and numerous small trials can be seen to have been made upon it. At about G.R. 2864.0153, well up and across from the mine dam, is Long Crag Level. Marked on the map, it is safe to enter and has been put in as a cross-cut for some 516 feet with about 332 feet of side drives. Seeking the Long Crag Vein the miners met with no luck; despite the strong appearance of it at the surface above here, there was little, if any, copper found in the mine and even quartz was something of a rarity! (See Fig. 53). Shades of Borlase Mine Bottom Level!

Below the gray spoil-heap note the rather large ruined shed. Examination will reveal the place where the blacksmith tested his harpened jumpers or drilling chisels. This was a favourite habit of smiths and similar little holes are to be seen outside the smithy down at the works.

A bearing of 310° down along the crag from the spoil-heap brings one to three small trial trenches which are probably on the western extremity of Pave York Vein. Well up above these three trenches -

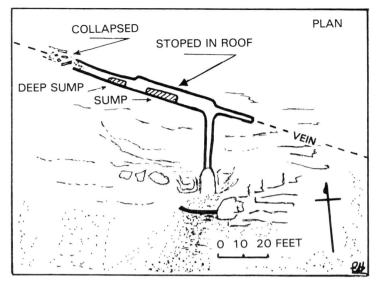

*Fig. 54*    *The mine on the outcrop of Long Crag Vein above*
          *Long Crag Level - Greenburn.*

higher even than Long Crag Level - there are some old workings on
the Long Crag Vein at surface, at about G.R. 2859.0147. Two
tunnels are still open, one having a dead tree in its entrance cut. It
runs in for a short distance, see Fig. 54, to where it is blocked by a
rock-fall. Although an interesting little mine, care is needed, for
there are deep flooded holes in the floor. The other working is less
easy to locate, is deep in water, has workings in floor and roof, and
too dangerous to explore. Other tunnels are suspected around this
site but have been buried by loose material.

Bearing in mind the depth at which magnetite made its presence felt
in the Bonsor Vein it can only be regarded as curious that the same
mineral was found here in these workings at this altitude. Of course it
is not known whether this ore continues in depth or was merely a
sporadic appearance here on the back of the vein - these were only
shallow workings.

## Route 7
# Seathwaite Copper Mine

Little more than passing reference has been given to this mine because of the dearth of documentary material. T.Eastwood does however, supply a fair amount of information, though he admits that no plans existed and that other material was hard to obtain.

The mine lies beyond, or N.E., of the partly artificial Seathwaite Tarn (Barrow-in-Furness water supply) and apart from the ruins of a few sheds, a short length of track connecting the lower, middle and top levels, and the spoil heaps, there is little to be seen. A private road has been constructed up to the waterworks but no cart track was ever taken to the mine itself. It is evident, therefore, that what ore was won, was hand dressed, pack-horsed to a cart track obscured by the dam road and then carted down to the nearest rail-head at Broughton-in-Furness.

Seathwaite Mine (not to be confused with the Seathwaite in Borrowdale) may be approached by a long drag up the dam road from the Duddon Valley or by climbing over the range due west of the Coniston Mines. You can see from the map that it is due west of Levers Water.

The level mouths are run-in or buried but one or two might be re-opened with a little effort. Indeed why not? Shepherds need have no worries if the entrance is made unattractive to sheep in winter. The tunnels are clearly indicated on our 6 inch maps and visually the spoil-heaps give them away.

T.Eastwood tells us that there are four East-West veins being probably part of the Coniston pattern. In addition to chalcopyrite, large quantities of black sulphide were found - chalcocite. The lowest level was driven 100 fathoms north to cut the Southern Vein, and levels were taken off east and west along it. The western branch, it appears, was taken along the vein for over 300 yards, cutting through a cross-course. Middle Level was put in north-north-east for 110 fathoms intersecting the Southern Vein 70-80 feet above Bottom Level. Its northern end cuts the Middle Vein.

Upper Level, was driven 100 fathoms, to bisect the two northern lodes.

# Glossary

ADIT      - tunnel driven into a fell-side to allow access to mineral vein as well as drainage and ventilation.

AIR-SHAFT      - vertical shaft to surface for ventilation, sometimes known as a smokehole.

BACKS      - vein and workings in the roof of a level.

BOULDER-CLAY      - glacial clay containing rounded pebbles to huge boulders.

BUDDLE      - to wash and separate ground ore from waste and also the various contrivances for this purpose.

CROSS-COURSE      - a fault cutting across a vein and often shifting it or cutting it off.

COUNTRY-ROCK      - or simply country. The rock in which the veins are found.

CROSS-CUT      - tunnel or level driven to intersect a vein at about right-angles.

CLOSE-HEAD      - underground slate quarry, often of great size.

DRIFT      - a tunnel or level.

ELECTRON      - light caving ladder with wire sides and alloy rungs.

FOSSICKING      - grubbing in waste heaps for any ore thrown away.

FATHOM      - six feet.

FAULT      - see cross-course.

HORSE (RIDER)      - barren section in middle of a split vein.

IRON-PYRITE      - natural compound of iron and sulphur often referred to as fool's gold.

JUMPER      - hand held drilling chisel of varying length.

JIGS      - machine for effecting separation of ground waste and ore using agitation in water, and gravity.

| JACK-ROLL | - also known as a windlass.... hand turned device for raising stuff from shallow depths. |
|---|---|
| KIBBLE | - mine bucket, often quite large, made of iron or wood and used for drawing stuff from shafts. |
| LEVEL | - see adit. |
| LODE | - vein carrying a mineral which may or may not be worth exploiting. |
| MISPICKEL | - natural compound of arsenic and sulphur. |
| MASONRY-ARCHED | - as implied, a tunnel arched with rock for support often in the soft ground at a tunnel mouth. |
| OLD MAN | - miners' term for abandoned workings, also used to describe miners of long ago. |
| OUTCROP | - a vein or lode of any sort where it comes to surface. |
| ORE-PASS | - a small shaft, or partitioned section in a shaft, or a stone lined narrow shaft down through loose waste packed around it and used solely for dropping ore down to a level below. |
| PELTON-WHEEL | - enclosed wheel with scoops on periphery turned by powerful water jet from a nozzle. |
| PLUG & FEATHERS | - tool consisting of two half-round tapering bars inserted in hole drilled several inches deep and forced apart by wedge driven in between them effecting thereby a splitting force. |
| RAISE or RISE | - an internal shaft being put upwards in the vein or country-rock. When this connects with a level above it can be known as a winze, a pass for ore or ladder, or even a sump. It depends upon the district and the miner. |
| RIDER | - see horse. |
| ROUND-BUDDLE | - a convex or concave device once used for sizing, washing and separating ground ore/stone. See also buddle. |

113

| | |
|---|---|
| RHYOLITE | - hard volcanic lava.... difficult to hand drill. |
| STOPE | - vertical excavation on the vein, below (underhand) or above (overhand) a level. These may be a few inches wide or enormous in size. |
| SUMP | - a pit sunk on a vein for a trial. If not drained it will fill with water. If connecting with a lower level it would be a winze for a man way, ore pass, or ventilation. A pit to collect water for the mine pump is also a sump. |
| SPOIL | - the rejected waste material from the mining and milling operations. |
| SHOT | - a blast using gunpowder or dynamite usually in a shothole, hence shot-firing. A miner was 'shot' when injured in an explosion. |
| SCREENING | - sizing the ore by passing it over spaced sloping bars or perforated steel sheet. |
| STAMPS | - the earlier grinding machines where heavy vertical wooden baulks shod with iron are lifted and dropped into mortars thus pounding the ore.... usually the lower grade stuff. |
| VEIN | - see lode |
| WINZE | - an internal shaft of small dimension connecting two or more levels together. See sump.... raise.... and ore-pass. |

\*   \*   \*

Mining terms varied from mine to mine and district to district. Often they were contradictory. The foregoing are therefore intended solely as a guide.

# *Index*

## OF SITES AND MINES

For use with Ordnance Survey sheets SD 29 NE, NY 20 SE and NY 30 SW, all being of Scale 1: 10,560 or 6 inches to one mile. These maps were decided upon because of their detail and ease of reading. Items are correlated in the same order in which they occur in the foregoing guide.

# OTHER READING

Two other books on the subject of mining are:-

Mining in the Lake Counties by W.T.Shaw.

Mines and Mining in the Lake District by John Postlethwaite.

Both contain additional material on Coniston Mines.

## LIGHTING - a hazard to equipment.

Good reliable lighting underground, be it in cave or mine, is vital. It needs to be in the form of a headlamp connected to a battery unit on a belt around the wearer's waist - thus the hands are kept free. Without the greatest of care, and sometimes despite it, certain acid (and alkaline) batteries leak their contents. This can not only cause skin burns but damage clothing, rucksacks etc. Far worse, threatening lethal consequences, is the insidious damage which can occur, often unnoticed, to ropes and slings and even electron ladders and belay wire, when acid comes into contact with them.

A unit which overcomes this threat has virtually superceded the old type of miner's lamp. The heart of the Speleo Technics FX2 battery pack is a pair of sealed nickel-cadmium cells which have an extremely long life and ability to be stored indefinitely in any state of charge or discharge. The battery is leak-proof and totally free from maintenance. It is enclosed in a tough abrasion resistant case and is much lighter and more compact than the clumsy batteries the miners had to carry. The battery is easily recharged and gives 10 hours bright light from a halogen bulb.

The unit is available from outdoor equipment shops, or direct from Speleo Technics, Victoria Mill, Mersey Street, Longridge, Preston PR3 3RN. Several specialist caving shops offer a hire service.

Further advice on suitable equipment and its use is best obtained from a good supplier and/or a reputable caving group. Or from climbing clubs for that matter.

# ACKNOWLEDGEMENT

The writer wishes to thank all friends and associates, too many to list individually, who over the years frequently accompanied him on surface and underground trips - sometimes patiently assisting on surveys in wet and uncomfortable conditions. He craves also to remind certain members and ex members of the Red Rose Cave and Pothole Club, of the exciting explorations in the latter part of the 1960's, and more recently, thrilling expeditions with colleagues (some of long standing) lately formed into Cumbria Amenity Trust - a mining history society.

# EPILOGUE

THE KNOCKERS ..... the kobolds, goblins or gins of the mine. The little unseen beings whose faint tappings could direct the miner to rich ore. Generally they were considered friendly, if mischievous, but beware he who failed to leave a few crumbs from his lunch box for them. Beware too, the one who whistled in the mine, or cursed or mocked them. In those cases ill-fortune, injury, or worse, could befall the errant miner.

The disposition of the KNOCKERS towards the present day intruders is not quite known for certain!

This book is dedicated to generations of miners who because of the dim light of their tallow candles never saw the huge size of their work.

## Coniston Copper - A History
### by Eric G. Holland

The definitive history of an outstanding industrial enterprise which lasted four centuries. Dozens of photographs, drawings and maps. A real collector's item.

ISBN 0 902363 42 5     312 pp     Hard back

CICERONE PRESS  2 Police Square, Milnthorpe, Cumbria, LA7 7PU